EASY

Dessert

C·O·O·K·I·N·G

WITH

5

INGREDIENTS
or less

Lia Roessner Wilson

Easy Dessert Cooking
With 5 Ingredients or Less

1st Printing   August 2003

Copyright © 2003
By Cookbook Resources LLC, Highland Village, Texas.
All rights reserved

ISBN 1-931294-43-7

Library of Congress Number: 2003105099

Edited, Designed, Published and Manufactured in the
United States of America by
Cookbook Resources, LLC
541 Doubletree Drive
Highland Village, Texas 75077
Toll free 866-229-2665
www.cookbookresources.com

Sweets From The Kitchen

This cookbook is not about getting necessary nutrition or watching calories. It is about necessary pleasure and happiness and about watching the pleasure and happiness of others.

It's about the real pleasure of cooking and eating. It is about DESSERTS.

The way we see it, desserts are probably essential to a healthy, psychological make-up. After all, what else helps us feel happy, excited, filled with good anticipation, satisfied and secure? Cookies can do it. Cakes can do it. Pies can certainly do it. And all those other sweets that make life good can certainly do it.

With every bite of a dessert, somewhere in the back of our minds, memories flash of special occasions, birthday cakes, homemade cookies, favorite pies. We go back to happy times before mortgages and kids and remember lives that were simple and chocolate made us happy.

Desserts make memories. And good memories, like good desserts, add to the happiness in our lives.

We hope these simple desserts give you a way to make memories in your own home. When life is especially hectic, we think reading or cooking the recipes in this cookbook will make your day better. And when you think about it, everyday is a little nicer, a little warmer and a little happier with a homemade dessert.

Contents

Sauces and Toppings 7

There is nothing better than an easy, flashy sauce to turn the ordinary dessert into an extraordinary dessert. With these sauces and toppings you are able to make the plainest dessert into the fanciest sweets.

Fruit Desserts 19

Cherries, strawberries, peaches, pears and more are sweetened, honeyed, spiced and soaked to offer fresh and canned fruits for desserts. Each recipe in this section has its own unique and delicious presentation of the best of fruits.

Frozen Desserts 35

Ice creams, sherbets, sorbets, granitas and gelatos are frozen delights for the best of refreshing summer and spring desserts. Frozen desserts were never so easy and so completely good.

Puddings and Custards 57

Puddings and custards blend the best of 5 ingredients or less to swirl together creamy, rich flavors. Fast and simple, these desserts are treats any time.

Cremes 65

Distinct creme brulees are flavored with peaches, maple and chocolate to offer a variety of classic favorites. Smooth and substantial, these cremes top the dessert ladder for lighter sweets.

Mousses 72

These light, but rich desserts come surrounded by ladyfingers, hidden under whipped cream and topped with nuts and fruit zest. They are wonderful and live up to their reputation of more sophisticated desserts.

Souffles 80

Sweet soufflés are baked, chilled and frozen and blend only the best purees, chocolates and liqueurs.

Parfaits 85

These delightful parfaits combine toffees, buttery shortcakes, creamy chocolates, fruits and puddings for extraordinary flavor.

Pies 89

Here are slices of the supreme in these perennial favorites. There are fruit pies, creamy pies, mochas, creme de menthe and more. All explode with flavor and variety.

Contents

Cheesecakes 110

Rich and creamy cheesecakes are easy and elegant. Make these a strawberry-topped, caramel covered cheesecakes and they will be everyone's favorites.

Cobblers and Crisps 113

Apricot, blueberry, peach and strawberries cobblers, crisps and crumbs make this an old-fashion delight.

Pastries 120

Paper-thin pastries are well matched to fruits and flavors fit for kings and queens.

Tart 134

Little pastry crusts are filled with custards and fruits for memorable endings to any meal.

Crepes 149

Thin tasty pancake-like pastries are filled with fresh fruits, creams and sauces for delicate tastes and special flavors.

Flaming Desserts 154

For the ultimate in sophistication, flaming desserts serve up special touches for special meals. These simple desserts look complicated and expensive, but are easy to prepare and elegant to serve.

Cookies 159

For the best in homemade, these cookie recipes are snaps. They are quick and easy and great for any time and any place.

Candies 210

Crunchy, nutty brittles, fudges, bites and clusters are fabulous for the taste and fabulous for the time.

Cakes 229

Pound cakes, butter cakes, chocolate cakes, old-fashion cakes, fresh berry cakes, trifles and tortes make this a spectacular source for fast and fabulous cakes.

Index 267

Order Form 287

Dessert Sauces

Easy Chocolate Sauce

½ cup heavy whipping cream
3 (1 ounce) squares semi-sweet baking chocolate

Combine whipping cream and chocolate in small saucepan.

Cook over low heat, stirring constantly, until chocolate melts and mixture is smooth and slightly thick.

Remove from heat and cool to room temperature.

If not used immediately, place in covered container and chill until ready to use.

Warm slightly in microwave if necessary before using.

Yields about ¾ cup.

Hot Fudge Sauce

2 cups chocolate chips
½ cup half-and-half
½ teaspoon vanilla

Combine chocolate chips and half-and-half in small saucepan over very low heat.

Stir constantly until chocolate melts and mixture is smooth.

Remove from heat and stir in vanilla. Serve warm.

Keep remaining sauce chilled.

When ready to use again, warm slightly in microwave and stir after every 30 seconds, until it can be poured.

Caramel Sauce

¼ cup sugar
3 tablespoons water
½ cup heavy whipping cream

Bring sugar and water to a boil, stirring frequently until sugar dissolves.

Simmer for about 10 minutes, swirling pan occasionally, until sugar mixture is deep amber color.

Remove from heat and quickly whisk in cream. Mixture will bubble furiously.

Return to medium heat, cook and stir until mixture thickens and lumps of caramel melt. Remove from heat and cool.

Boysenberry Sauce

1 (16 ounce) bag frozen, unsweetened boysenberries, thawed
½ cup sugar
1 tablespoon lemon juice
1 tablespoon cornstarch

Place boysenberries, sugar and lemon juice in small heavy saucepan.

Cook and stir over medium heat to soften berries and release juice.

Strain mixture into small bowl and crush berries with back of spoon to strain out solids.

Discard solids and pour juice back into saucepan.

Remove 2 tablespoons juice and mix with cornstarch to make a paste. Stir into juice.

Cook and stir over medium heat until it thickens, about 4 to 5 minutes. Cover and chill until ready to serve.

Makes about 1 cup.

Raspberry Sauce

Serve this homemade raspberry sauce over ice cream, cake or pudding.

1 (12 ounce) bag frozen sweetened raspberries, thawed
¼ cup orange juice
1 tablespoon cornstarch
¼ cup sugar

Puree raspberries using a food processor or blender. Strain seeds and solids and discard.

Put puree in medium saucepan.

Dissolve cornstarch into small amount of orange juice and stir until smooth.

Add to puree in pan with remaining orange juice and sugar.

Bring to boil over medium heat and cook, stirring constantly, for 1 to 2 minutes until it thickens. Remove from heat and cool.

Makes about 1 cup.

Tip: Put this sauce in a syrup dispenser and serve it on pancakes and waffles. It is wonderful!

Rum Sauce

This delightful buttery, caramel sauce is lightly flavored with rum and goes well with a variety of fruits and desserts. Serve it warm over apple cobbler, pound cake or ice cream.

6 tablespoons butter
½ cup firmly packed light brown sugar
3 tablespoons heavy whipping cream, divided
1 tablespoon light rum

Melt butter in medium saucepan over medium heat.

Stir in brown sugar and cook, stirring frequently, until mixture is thick and bubbly, about 5 minutes.

Add cream 1 tablespoon at a time, stirring well after each addition.

Stir and cook until sugar dissolves and mixture is smooth, about 3 minutes.

Stir in rum and cook about 1 more minute.

Remove from heat and serve warm over ice cream, apple or peach cobblers.

Creamy Fruit Topping

Use this tasty topping as an accompaniment for different fruits.
Consider making a fruit tray with raspberries, strawberries and pineapple
and serve the topping as a dip.

1 pint heavy whipping cream
1 cup sugar
1 packet unflavored gelatin
1 pint sour cream
1 teaspoon vanilla

In medium saucepan, heat cream, sugar and gelatin until gelatin dissolves.

Remove mixture from heat and let cool to lukewarm. Chill until mixture begins to set.

Fold in sour cream and vanilla. Chill until ready to serve.

Serve with fresh sliced fruit.

Whipped Cream

1 cup heavy (whipping) cream
4 tablespoons sugar
2 teaspoons vanilla extract

In medium bowl, beat cream on medium-low speed for about 30 seconds.

Increase speed to medium-high and slowly add sugar and vanilla.

Continue to beat until soft peaks form.

Hot Spiced Apples Topping

2 tablespoons butter
2 tablespoons brown sugar
½ teaspoon apple pie spice or cinnamon
1 (21 ounce) can apple pie filling
½ cup chopped walnuts, toasted

In medium saucepan, melt butter and stir in brown sugar, apple pie spice and pie filling.

Bring to boil and remove from heat. Stir in walnuts.

Serve warm over ice cream or crepes.

Whiskey Cream

Try this with pecan pie!

2 cups heavy whipping cream
1 cup honey
½ cup whiskey

In well chilled, medium bowl, beat cream until stiff peaks form.

In separate bowl, combine honey with whiskey. Fold gently into whipped cream.

Cover and chill for several hours.

Island-Pineapple Sauce

1 (20 ounce) can pineapple pie filling
¼ cup curacao or orange liqueur
1 tablespoon lemon juice
1 tablespoon orange zest

In small saucepan over medium heat, combine pie filling, liqueur, lemon juice and orange zest.

Bring to boil and stir constantly.

Serve over ice cream or pound cake.

Sunny Lemon Sauce

1 (20 ounce) can pineapple pie filling
¼ cup lemon juice
6 whole cloves

In medium saucepan over medium heat, combine pie filling, lemon juice and cloves.

Simmer for 10 minutes. Remove cloves.

Serve over ice or pound cake.

Peanutty Ice Cream Crunch

Peanut Butter Sauce

1 cup peanut butter chips
⅓ cup milk
¼ cup whipping cream
¼ teaspoon vanilla

In medium saucepan, over low heat melt peanut butter chips with milk and whipping cream and stir constantly until mixture is smooth.

Remove from heat and stir in vanilla. Cool to room temperature

Coconut Crunch

½ cup flaked coconut
½ cup chopped nuts
1 tablespoon butter

Preheat oven to 325°.

Combine coconut, nuts and butter in small baking dish. Toast in oven 6 to 8 minutes and stir occasionally. (Watch so mixture does not burn.)

In 4 dessert dishes place a scoop ice cream in each.

Spoon peanut butter sauce over top and sprinkle with coconut crunch.

Candied Almond Topping

This easy candied almond recipe gives you a nice alternative to plain nuts as topping for ice cream and other desserts.

2 tablespoons water
⅓ cup sugar
½ cup slivered almonds, toasted

Line baking sheet with aluminum foil.

Bring water and sugar to boil in small heavy saucepan.

Without stirring, cook over medium high heat until mixture becomes deep amber color, about 10 minutes, occasionally wash down sides of pan with wet pastry brush.

Remove from heat and stir in almonds. Quickly spread mixture on prepared baking sheet.

Cool to harden, break into small pieces and store in airtight container.

Tip: To toast the almonds, place in single layer on baking sheet and bake at 350° until golden brown, about 5 minutes. Remove from oven and cool.

Warm Walnut Sauce

1 cup sugar
1 teaspoon fresh lemon juice
⅓ cup water
½ cup chopped walnuts
½ cup whipping cream

In medium saucepan, stir together sugar, lemon juice and water and cook over medium heat, stirring constantly, until sugar dissolves.

Over medium high heat, continue to cook and stir until mixture turns an amber color.

Add walnuts and continue to cook and stir for about 1 minute.

Remove from heat and slowly pour in cream while stirring. Continue to stir until sauce is well blended and slightly thicker.

Pour over ice cream, cake or brownies.

Toffee Crunch

½ cup sugar
1½ teaspoons light corn syrup
6 tablespoons (¾ stick) butter
2 tablespoons water

Lightly grease 9 x 13-inch baking pan.

In small saucepan stir together sugar, corn syrup, butter and water.

Over medium-high heat, bring to a boil and cook, stirring constantly, until sugar dissolves.

Continue to boil without stirring until temperature reaches 300° on candy thermometer and mixture turns a golden brown color.

Pour mixture onto baking sheet to cool. When toffee is cool and hard, break into small pieces and put over ice cream, cake or brownies.

Fruit

Cherries

Selecting

Cherries are harvested when ripe and do not ripen significantly once picked. When you buy sweet cherries, look for large, plump, smooth and dark-colored fruit because the darker the cherry, the sweeter the flavor. Avoid any that are sticky, bruised, extremely soft or have shriveled stems which are signs of age. Also try to pick cherries with stems attached. Once stems are removed, the cherries spoil more quickly.

Both sweet and sour cherries are available pitted and canned, packed in water or syrup or frozen. When possible, use fresh sweet cherries instead of canned. One pound of fresh cherries can replace 1-pound can sour cherries. Once they have been pitted, fresh cherries will yield the same 2 cups that the can holds.

Storing

Put fresh cherries in a plastic bag and refrigerate immediately. Use within 3 days. Canned cherries will keep for 1 year unopened in a cool, dark cupboard. After opening the can, transfer the cherries to a covered glass, plastic or ceramic container and refrigerate for up to 1 week.

Preparing

If using fresh cherries in pies or other baked dishes, pit fruit with a cherry pitter or small, sharp knife. Operating like a hole punch, a cherry pitter makes fast work of an otherwise tedious task. Simply place a stemmed cherry in the pitter and then squeeze the handle. The tool extracts the pit while leaving the fruit whole. Once you use one, you will wonder how you ever lived without it.

Brandied Cherries

You cannot beat this simple dessert when you want to enjoy ripe cherries in the peak of the season. If you like, you may also add an apricot or two with the cherries for a little variety.

½ cup sugar
¼ brandy
2 pounds cherries, pitted
2 tablespoons lemon juice

Combine sugar and brandy in medium saucepan.

Add cherries and the lemon juice. Bring to simmer, stirring occasionally, until sugar dissolves.

Cook cherries over medium heat until tender, about 5 minutes.

Serve warm over ice cream or angel food cake.

Bing Cherry Shortcakes

½ pound bing cherries, pitted
½ cup water
½ cup plus 2 tablespoons sugar
⅔ cup heavy whipping cream
2 tablespoons cherry liqueur
4 sponge cakes

Bring cherries, water and ½ cup sugar to simmer in medium saucepan and cook for 4 to 5 minutes. Remove from heat and let cool.

In chilled bowl, whip cream, remaining 2 tablespoons sugar and cherry liqueur until stiff peaks form.

Spoon cherries and syrup over each shortcake and top with whipped cream mixture before serving.

Strawberries Topped with Sweetened Mascarpone

This simple, 5-minute dessert is refreshing and delicious, especially when made with flavorful, ripe strawberries. It is an excellent end to a hearty meal.

1 cup whipping cream, chilled
½ cup mascarpone cheese, softened
¼ cup sugar
2 tablespoons sweet Marsala wine
1 pound fresh strawberries, hulled, thickly quartered

In mixing bowl, combine whipping cream, mascarpone cheese, sugar and wine.

Beat on high speed until soft peaks form.

Divide strawberries between 6 to 8 custard cups or dessert cups. Top with cheese mixture divided equally among the dessert cups.

Makes 2 cups.

Tip: If you can't find mascarpone, you may substitute Neufchatel or cream cheese.

Strawberries in Chocolate Tuxedos

For a special occasion, dress up some strawberries in bittersweet and white chocolate suits. They are easy to make, but look very sophisticated and elegant.

**4 ounces white baking chocolate
2 teaspoons cooking oil, divided
1 pound fresh strawberries with stems, washed, dried
4 ounces bittersweet or semi-sweet baking chocolate**

**Equipment Needed:
2-tined fork or toothpicks for dipping strawberries
Pastry bag or small parchment bag
Small pastry tip (size 1 or 2)**

In top of double boiler over simmering water, combine white chocolate and 1 teaspoon oil. Stir until chocolate melts and is smooth. Transfer chocolate to small, deep bowl or other container.

Use fingers or 2-tined fork to grasp each strawberry at crown and dip into white chocolate until chocolate just reaches crown. Place on wax paper or aluminum foil to set chocolate. Chill to speed process.

When white chocolate is set, place bittersweet chocolate and remaining teaspoon of oil in top of double boiler that has been washed and dried thoroughly and set over simmering water.

Melt bittersweet chocolate, stirring constantly, until smooth.

Transfer chocolate to small deep bowl and carefully dip "shoulders" of each strawberry in bittersweet chocolate. Do 1 side first and then other. Dip at angle so white chocolate looks like triangle in middle of strawberry's front.

Place small piece of unmelted chocolate in remaining melted chocolate and stir to cool melted chocolate a little.

(continued on next page)

(continued)

Put melted chocolate into pastry bag with small tip (size 1 or 2) and make 3 dots in row to form "buttons" above point of triangle. Leave room for bowtie above them.

To make bowtie, pipe 2 small triangles with points meeting in middle, just above top button. Fill them with chocolate. They should look like little bowties.

Place strawberries back on wax paper or foil and let chocolate set. Chill until ready to serve.

Yields about 2 dozen.

Tips:

Make sure that strawberries are perfectly dry and at room temperature.

Do not let ANY water touch chocolate while it is melting in double boiler or it will seize.

If bowties are a problem, do not add them. The strawberries will still look great with the buttons and "suits".

When you fill pastry bag, twist top above chocolate and use gentle pressure to pipe chocolate onto strawberries. When you have made your button or outline of bowtie, release pressure on bag before you lift it up.

To pipe bowties, make sharp figure eights. Start to left of button and pipe downward. Stop and pipe at diagonal to right of button. Stop and pipe downward and at diagonal to top left, where you began. Simply fill each half of bowtie.

* If you don't have pastry bag and tip, use resealable plastic sandwich bag. Fill it with melted chocolate, twist above chocolate, and snip tiny piece of 1 corner. Apply gentle pressure to dispense chocolate.

Wine-Soaked Nectarines

1¾ cups white Zinfandel or Riesling wine
¼ cup sugar
6 large nectarines, halved, pitted
1 pint raspberries, washed, dried

In large bowl, stir sugar into wine until dissolved. Slice nectarines into ¼-inch pieces.

Gently place nectarines and raspberries in mixture.

Cover and let stand at room temperature for at least 2 hours before serving.

Chill for up to 6 hours. Bring to room temperature before serving.

Sugared Peaches with Sweet Marsala Wine Sauce

What a great way to enjoy fresh peaches! Sweet tender peaches are covered in a delicate wine sauce flavored with tiny currants.

¼ cup dried currants
½ cup orange juice
½ cup sweet Marsala wine
6 tablespoons sugar, divided
2 large peaches, peeled, pitted, sliced into ¼-inch slices

Place currants, orange juice, wine and 4 tablespoons sugar in medium saucepan.

Bring to boil and cook, stirring frequently, over medium heat until syrupy about 10 minutes.

While sauce is cooking, place peaches in shallow baking dish or on a tray.

Sprinkle with remaining 2 tablespoons sugar and place under broiler.

Broil for 2 to 3 minutes until sugar melts and slightly browns. (Watch carefully so they don't burn.) Remove from oven.

Place peach slices on plate, drizzle sauce over slices and serve.

Serves 4.

Optional: To add even more flavor to this dish, put a cinnamon stick in sauce with other ingredients and discard it when sauce is removed from heat.

Apple-Spiced Pears

4 medium pears
½ cup firmly packed brown sugar
¼ cup water
1 teaspoon apple pie spice

Preheat oven to 350°.

Peel and core pears. Slice in half vertically and place in 9 x 13-inch baking dish.

Score each pear by making 6 or 7 vertical and horizontal slices and set aside.

In small saucepan, combine brown sugar, water and apple pie spice. Cook over medium heat until sugar dissolves.

Pour over pears. Cover with foil and bake for 45 minutes.

Remove from oven. Cool, pour syrup over pears and serve.

Honeyed Pears

2 (16 ounce) cans pear halves, drained
½ cup honey
¼ cup butter, melted
1 cup macaroons or butter cookies, crushed

Preheat oven to 350°.

Place pear halves in single layer in 11 x 7-inch or 9 x 9-inch baking dish.

In small bowl, combine butter with honey and pour over pears.

Bake, uncovered, for 20 minutes.

Sprinkle crushed cookies over pears and bake for another 10 minutes. Serve warm.

Pears Poached in Wine

4 firm, ripe pears
2 tablespoons lemon juice
1 cup sweet Marsala wine
2 cups hot water
⅓ cup sugar

Peel pears and carefully remove core from bottom end leaving stem end intact. Set aside.

Combine lemon juice, wine, hot water and sugar in 2-quart saucepan. Bring liquid to boil and add pears standing with stem up. Add enough hot water, if necessary, to make liquid just cover pears.

Return to boil and simmer, covered, for about 15 minutes or until pears are tender. Remove pears and place in dish with high sides.

Return liquid to rapid boil and reduce to about 1 cup. This may take about 30 minutes, depending upon how much liquid is used.

Pour over pears and cool. Serve at room temperature or chilled.

Cherry Delight

This is a great fruity dessert and it only takes 5 minutes to make.

1 (20 ounce) can cherry pie filling
1 (11 ounce) can mandarin oranges, drained
¼ cup chopped pecans
1 (20 ounce) can pineapple chunks, drained, juice reserved
2 bananas, sliced, dipped in reserved pineapple juice

Gently combine all ingredients.

Chill for 1 hour.

Tip: This dessert is best served chilled, so if you want to make it just before serving, you should chill all the ingredients beforehand.

Stained Glass Salad

1 (11 ounce) can mandarin oranges, drained
1 (10 ounce) package frozen strawberries, thawed
1 (8 ounce) can pineapple tidbits, drained
1 (20 ounce) can pears, sliced, drained
1 (20 ounce) can peach pie filling

Pour all fruit into serving bowl and chill.

Serve over pound cake or by itself in dessert dishes.

Not-So-Sweet Dessert Salad

To have this dessert ready in 5 minutes, chill all the ingredients first. When it is time to serve, just combine and you're ready to go!

**1 (1 pint) carton cottage cheese, drained
1 (8 ounce) carton frozen whipped topping, thawed
½ cup chopped pecans
1 (20 ounce) can chunk pineapple, drained
1 (11 ounce) can mandarin oranges, drained**

Combine cottage cheese and frozen whipped topping in large bowl. Mix until well blended.

Stir in pecans.

Fold in pineapple and oranges.

Fresh Fruit With Hawaiian Glaze

You choose the fresh fruit you enjoy most: bananas, strawberries, pineapple, melon, kiwi, nectarines, peaches, apples, grapes and more. Add the Hawaiian Glaze below for a beautiful, refreshing dessert.

Hawaiian Glaze

1 lemon
2 cups pineapple or orange-pineapple juice
3 tablespoons sugar
1 tablespoon cornstarch
Whipped cream

Squeeze 1 tablespoon juice from lemon and grate peel to yield ½ teaspoon. Set aside.

In medium saucepan, combine pineapple juice, sugar, cornstarch, lemon juice and lemon peel.

Cook over medium-high heat and bring to boil.

Reduce heat and continue to cook until sauce begins to thicken.

Arrange fruit slices in individual cups and pour sauce, warm or chilled, over fruit. Top with whipped cream.

Red, White and Gooey Banana Splits

Sometimes we forget the simplest things, so we added this to our collection. The fun part is in the variations we suggest and you invent.

1 firm banana
1 scoop each: vanilla, chocolate, strawberry ice cream
2 tablespoons each: chocolate syrup,
strawberry syrup, butterscotch sauce
Whipped cream
Maraschino cherries

Peel banana and slice in 2 pieces lengthwise.

Put 1 scoop each of vanilla, chocolate and strawberry ice cream between slice of banana.

Pour chocolate syrup, strawberry syrup and butterscotch sauce over scoops of ice cream.

Top with whipped cream and maraschino cherry.

Optional: Finely chopped nuts sprinkled over the top are really great!

Variations: Try neopolitan ice cream instead of chocolate, vanilla and strawberry.

Invent your own special ice cream and topping selections. Top with sprinkles, Red Hots, chocolate chips, peanut butter chips, brickle chips, M & M's, candy bars, cookies, almond slivers and the list goes on. What will you come up with to make this a memorable dessert?

Frozen Desserts

Ice cream, sorbet, granite, granita and sherbet!

What is the difference between these popular frozen desserts that we hear about and enjoy so often?

Ice cream is actually a frozen custard made from eggs, dairy and sugar containing at least 8 percent milk fat. Depending upon how much air is whipped into it, it can be fairly soft to very firm.

Sorbet [sor-BAY] is made from natural fruit juices and purees blended with sugar and water. It contains no milk or cream and has a softer consistency than sherbet.

Its counterpart is called **granité** in France and **granita** in Italy; however, these versions typically have a more granular texture than sorbet. Sorbet is churned until smooth, resulting in a creamy texture. **Granita** is scraped so it becomes icy and slushy.

Sherbet [SHER-biht] is a cross between sorbet and ice cream. It is creamy, smooth and made from fruit purees and juices, but it also contains some milk or cream, although in much smaller amounts than in ice cream. It owes its origins to the Middle East where a drink called charbet, made of sweetened fruit juice and water, was being made almost before recorded history.

Ice Creams

You may still make ice cream even if you do not own an ice cream maker! It will take slightly longer, but you may use the still-freeze method to freeze the ice cream mixture in your freezer.

It is simple. To prepare an ice cream mixture, place it in a mixing bowl or shallow dish (a shallow, metal pan works best), cover and put in the freezer. When it is firm around the edges, but still slushy in the middle, (usually about 20 to 45 minutes), remove the pan and stir the mixture with a wooden spoon or whisk.

Return to the freezer until the mixture is again firm around edges. Repeat this step 1 or 2 more times until it is uniformly frozen the last time. If you get a hard freeze, let the mixture soften slightly in the refrigerator before serving.

Ice cream made with the still-freeze method will not be as smooth as ice cream made in an ice cream maker, but it is a great way to enjoy frozen desserts you want to make yourself.

The still-freeze method may be used for ice creams, sorbets, sherbets and granitas. Homemade always adds a special touch to any meal and everyone who enjoys it feels special.

Old-Fashion Ice Cream

2 cups light cream or half-and-half, divided
¾ cup sugar
1 cup whipping cream
2 teaspoons vanilla extract
2 teaspoons fresh lemon juice

In a small saucepan over low heat, cook 1 cup light cream and sugar. Stir until sugar dissolves.

Pour mixture into ovenproof bowl and cool to room temperature.

Pour in remaining light cream, whipping cream, vanilla and lemon juice. Cover and chill at least 3 hours.

Pour mixture into 1½-quart ice cream freezer and freeze according to manufacturer's directions.

Makes 1 quart.

Optional: Add 3 large, peeled, chopped peaches or 1 pound frozen peaches to ice cream. Set aside several pieces of peaches and put remaining fruit in blender and puree to. Add to ice cream before freezing.

Optional: Add 1 cup crushed cookies or candy bars just before freezing. Save some of the crushed cookies or candy for topping before serving.

Dark, Rich Chocolate Ice Cream

3 egg yolks
5 ounces bittersweet chocolate
1¾ cups milk
½ cup sugar
1 cup whipping cream

Whisk egg yolks until well beaten and set aside.

Chop chocolate into small pieces.

In medium heavy saucepan, combine milk and sugar. Cook over medium heat until mixture comes to a slow boil.

Whisk about ½ cup hot milk mixture into egg yolks. Whisk egg yolk mixture back into hot milk mixture in saucepan.

Cook over medium low heat, whisking constantly, for 2 minutes until mixture thickens slightly. Remove from heat.

Add chocolate and stir until chocolate melts.

Stir in cream. Cool at room temperature for 30 minutes and chill about 30 minutes.

Freeze in ice cream maker according to manufacturer's directions or use the still-freeze method described on page 37.

Toffee Ice Cream Delight

**3 cups (28 cookies) crushed cream-filled chocolate sandwich
cookies
3 tablespoons butter or margarine, melted
½ gallon French vanilla ice cream, softened, divided
1 (8 ounce) package milk chocolate toffee bits or 1⅓ cups crushed
chocolate-covered toffee candy bars, divided
1 (16 ounce) jar hot fudge topping**

Preheat oven to 350°.

In large bowl, combine cookie crumbs and butter. Mix well and press into bottom of ungreased 9 x 13-inch baking dish.

Bake for 5 minutes. Remove from oven and cool.

Carefully spread half of ice cream over cookie crust and sprinkle with half toffee.

Spread remaining ice cream over toffee and sprinkle with remaining toffee.

Cover and freeze until firm. Spread fudge topping over top of ice cream and keep frozen until ready to serve.

Chocolate Marshmallow Ice Cream Pie

2 cups miniature marshmallows
8 ounces chocolate, grated, divided
1 (5 ounce) can evaporated milk
1 (9 ounce) deep-dish, graham cracker pie crust
1 quart vanilla ice cream, softened

Place marshmallows, 6 ounces chocolate and evaporated milk in medium heavy saucepan.

Cook and stir over medium heat until marshmallows melt. Remove from heat and cool.

Spoon half mixture into prepared crust. Spread half ice cream over marshmallow mixture.

Spoon remaining half marshmallow mixture over ice cream and top with remaining ice cream.

Sprinkle pie with remaining grated chocolate. Cover with plastic wrap and freeze until firm.

Let stand at room temperature for 15 minutes to soften before serving.

Layered Ice Cream Treat

2 (3 ounce) packages ladyfingers
2 pints premium chocolate-chocolate chip ice cream, softened
2 pints premium vanilla ice cream, softened
1 (12 ounce) jar caramel sauce
1 (12 ounce) jar fudge topping

Split ladyfingers and layer in bottom of 9-inch springform pan.

Stand additional ladyfingers on end with sides touching, around inside edge of pan to look like crown. Use any leftover ladyfingers to fill in bare spaces in bottom of pan, breaking them into pieces if necessary.

Work quickly to spread chocolate-chocolate chip ice cream evenly over ladyfingers. Place in freezer until frozen.

Spread caramel sauce over chocolate ice cream and freeze again.

Spread vanilla ice cream evenly over hardened caramel sauce and freeze again.

Spread fudge topping over vanilla ice cream and place back in freezer until ready to serve.

To serve, take dessert out of mold and use sharp knife to cut slices.

Butter Pecan-Pumpkin Parfait

Try this for a change in the fall. It is a fun chilled dessert at any time.

1 (20 ounce) can pumpkin pie filling
1 quart vanilla or butter pecan ice cream
½ cup flaked coconut
½ cup finely chopped pecans
Dash nutmeg and cinnamon

Chill pumpkin pie filling overnight.

Just before serving, carefully spoon about 2 tablespoons pie filling into each of 6 parfait glasses.

Add small scoop of ice cream and sprinkle toasted coconut and chopped pecans. Repeat layers

Top with dash of nutmeg and cinnamon over last layer of ice cream.

Top with coconut and pecans.

Sweet Apricot Alaska

This really is easier than it may appear and it may be prepared the day before serving.

1 (18 ounce) box yellow cake mix
1 (20 ounce) can apricot pie filling
¼ cup apricot brandy
1 quart vanilla ice cream, softened
5 egg whites
⅔ cup sugar

Prepare and bake 2 (9-inch) cake layers according to package directions. Cool.

In small bowl, drain pie filling and reserve syrup.

Stir brandy into syrup, cover and chill.

In large bowl, crush apricots and fold into ice cream.

Pour into foil-lined 1½-quart bowl and freeze 3 hours or until firm.

Place 1 cake layer on foil-covered baking sheet. Freeze remaining cake layer for future use.

Take ice cream mixture out of mold and put onto cake. Remove foil from ice cream and return to freezer.

Preheat oven to 500°.

In large bowl, beat egg whites until soft peaks form.

Gradually add sugar and beat until stiff peaks form.

Completely cover cake and ice cream with meringue and seal it to foil on baking sheet.

Bake for 3 minutes or until lightly browned.

Trim foil to edge of meringue. Transfer cake to serving plate.

Serve immediately with chilled apricot brandy sauce.

Tip: Assemble Alaska and freeze the day before serving. Brown just before serving.

Frozen Mocha Ganache

This is a layered ice cream dessert encased within a soft,
chocolate coating and is sure to please.

2 pints premium coffee ice cream, softened
1 pint premium chocolate-chocolate chip ice cream, softened
1 cup heavy whipping cream, divided
3 tablespoons light corn syrup
2 (8 ounce) packages semi-sweet baking chocolate, chopped

Spread 1 pint coffee ice cream in 9 x 5-inch baking pan, evenly covering bottom and coming up sides. Freeze until firm.

Spread chocolate-chocolate chip ice cream evenly over coffee ice cream in bottom of baking pan. Freeze again until firm.

Spread remaining 1 pint coffee ice cream over chocolate chip ice cream, making surface as even as possible. Chocolate-chocolate chip ice cream is completely enclosed in the coffee ice cream. Freeze until solid.

In medium saucepan, combine ¾ cup whipping cream and corn syrup to make the ganache. Bring to simmer and remove from heat.

Whisk in chocolate until mixture is smooth. Cool until mixture thickens. Remove ¾ cup and set aside.

Turn ice cream out of baking pan. Work quickly to spread cooled ganache evenly over sides and top of ice cream. Return to freezer for at least 1 hour to set or until ready to serve.

Slice ice cream loaf using sharp knife. When ready to serve, combine remaining ¼ cup whipping cream with ¾ cup remaining ganache, mix well and warm. Spoon over ice cream servings.

Ganache is the rich chocolate icing used in this recipe. It is made by melting chocolate in whipping cream.

Tips: Add toasted almonds to top of ice cream loaf before serving. Warm knife under hot water and dry before cutting.

Raspberry Sherbet

1 (3.4 ounce) package dry raspberry gelatin
1 cup hot water
1 cup orange juice
2 tablespoons lemon juice
¾ cups sugar
2 cups milk

In large bowl, combine gelatin and hot water and stir to dissolve.

Add orange juice, lemon juice and sugar and stir to blend.

Chill until mixture thickens and becomes syrupy.

Stir in milk and freeze until mixture becomes mushy, about 2 hours.

Remove from freezer, beat until smooth and refreeze another several hours before serving.

Fresh Lime Sherbet

**1 (3 ounce) package dry lime gelatin
1 cup hot water
3 small limes
½ cup sugar
1½ cups milk
1 (13 ounce) can evaporated milk**

Dissolve gelatin in hot water. Stir in sugar until dissolved.

Squeeze ¼ cup juice from limes and grate peel to yield 2 tablespoons zest.

Stir in remaining ingredients. Pour into 8-inch square pan.

Freeze for about 2 hours or until mixture becomes mushy. Remove from freezer; then beat until smooth and refreeze.

Peach Sherbet

**2 cups frozen unsweetened peaches, sliced, partially thawed
½ cup plain nonfat yogurt
2 tablespoons orange juice concentrate
¼ cup sugar**

Puree peaches in food processor or blender.

Add yogurt, orange juice concentrate and sugar. Blend until mixture is creamy.

Put in square, freezer-safe pan and freeze about 2 hours until mixture becomes mushy. Remove from freezer; then beat until smooth and refreeze.

Cantaloupe Sherbet

1 large cantaloupe, peeled, seeded, cubed
1 (14 ounce) can sweetened condensed milk
2 tablespoons honey
1 tablespoon lemon juice

Combine cantaloupe, sweetened condensed milk, honey and lemon juice in food processor or blender. Blend until smooth.

Freeze in ice cream maker according to manufacturer's instructions or put mixture in square, freezer-safe pan and freeze for about 2 hours, until mixture becomes mushy.

Remove from freezer, beat until smooth and refreeze.

Cranberry-Chardonnay Sorbet

This is absolutely delicious and makes a refreshing summer dessert. It has a beautiful dark red color and very sweet, bold taste.

4 cups fresh or frozen cranberries
2 cups sugar
2 cups orange juice
1 cup Chardonnay or other white wine

Combine cranberries, sugar and orange juice in medium saucepan.

Bring to simmer and cook until cranberries are very soft, about 5 minutes.

Cool mixture and puree in food processor or blender. Stir in wine.

Pour into freezer container. Place in freezer until half frozen.

Remove from freezer and place in large bowl. Beat until mixture is smooth.

Return to freezer container and freeze until firm.

Pina Colada Sorbet

1 (15 ounce) can cream of coconut
¼ cup cold water
1 (8 ounce) can crushed pineapple with juice
3 tablespoons rum

Mix all ingredients in medium bowl and transfer to shallow baking dish, about 11 x 7 x 2-inch.

Cover and freeze, stirring every 30 minutes, until mixture is frozen, about 3 hours.

Keep covered and frozen until ready to serve. This may be stored for several days.

Tip: Cream of coconut is in liquor or drink mix section of most grocery stores.

Orange Sorbet

1 cup water
¼ cup sugar
⅓ cup honey
2 cups fresh orange juice

Combine water, sugar and honey in medium saucepan.

Bring to simmer, stirring occasionally until sugar dissolves.

Let mixture simmer uncovered for about 10 minutes until it becomes syrupy. Cool slightly.

Stir in orange juice.

Freeze in ice cream maker according to manufacturer's instructions or place in shallow baking dish in freezer, stirring every hour for 2 hours. Freeze until firm.

Grape Granita

Just like a snow cone...only better.

½ cup sugar
1 cup water
2 cups grape juice
1 cup ginger ale

Combine sugar and water in medium saucepan, bring to boil and stir until sugar dissolves. Boil for 15 minutes to make syrup.

Remove from heat and let cool. Stir in grape juice and ginger ale.

Pour mixture into 9 x 13-inch baking dish. Cover and freeze.

Stir every hour until mixture is frozen. Scrape with fork and place in dessert cups.

Tip: Make ice cream even if you do not own an ice cream maker! It will take slightly longer, but the still-freeze method will work in your freezer. See page 37 for instructions.

Chocolate-Chocolate Gelato

6 cups milk, divided
1⅓ cups sugar
12 eggs yolks, beaten
6 ounces semi-sweet chocolate, melted
6 ounces white chocolate baking bar, chopped

In large saucepan over medium heat, cook 3 cups milk, sugar and egg yolks, stirring occasionally, until mixture coats metal spoon.

Remove from heat and pour in melted chocolate. Whisk until smooth and add remaining milk. Stir to mix.

Cover with plastic wrap and chill overnight.

Stir in chopped white chocolate and freeze in 4-quart ice cream freezer according to manufacturer's directions.

Makes 2½ quarts.

Tip: See meringues to use egg whites.

Icy Pineapple Freeze

1 (20 ounce) can crushed pineapple and juice
½ cup sugar
1 (16 ounce) carton fat-free yogurt
½ teaspoon vanilla

In blender puree crushed pineapple and juice until smooth.

Pour into large bowl and stir in sugar. Let stand for 15 minutes for sugar to dissolve.

Add yogurt and vanilla and mix well.

Pour mixture into 1½-quart freezer container and freeze according to manufacturer's directions.

Cherry-Pineapple Freeze

**1 (13 ounce) can pineapple tidbits
1 (20 ounce) can cherry pie filling
1 (14 ounce) can sweetened condensed milk
2 cups whipped topping**

Drain pineapple tidbits and reserve syrup.

In large bowl, combine pie filling, sweetened condensed milk and pineapple.

Fold in whipped topping.

Spoon mixture into paper-lined muffin pans and freeze.

Remove from muffin pans and paper cups.

Serve on saucers or individual dishes and drizzle syrup over top.

Mint Special

1 tablespoon butter or margarine
20 chocolate sandwich cookies, crushed, divided
1 pint heavy whipping cream
1¾ cups colored after-dinner mints
4 cups miniature marshmallows

Butter 9 x 13-inch baking. Reserve ½ cup crushed cookies and set aside.

In chilled, medium bowl, beat whipping cream until stiff peaks form.

Fold mints and marshmallows into whipped cream. Spread carefully over cookie crumbs in baking dish.

Sprinkle remaining ½ cup cookie crumbs over top. Chill 8 hours or overnight.

Puddings & Custards

Crispy-Topped Pudding

2 cups flaked coconut
1 cup (2 sticks) butter or margarine, melted
2 cups flour
½ cup sugar
2 (22 ounce) containers chocolate or vanilla pudding

Preheat oven to 300°.

Combine coconut, butter, flour and sugar and pour in 9 x 13-inch baking pan.

Bake for 45 minutes, stirring every 10 minutes. Mixture will be crumbly.

Remove from oven and set aside half mixture for topping.

Spread pudding over crumbs and smooth. Sprinkle leftover crumb mixture on top.

Chill before serving.

Cinnamon-Orange Custard

1 large orange
⅔ cup sugar
7 egg yolks
2 cups heavy whipping cream, divided
¼ teaspoon cinnamon

Preheat oven to 325°.

Place 5 (6 ounce) ramekins in 9 x 13-inch baking dish.

Grate orange peel to yield 1 tablespoon zest. Squeeze orange to yield ¼ cup juice and set aside.

In medium bowl, lightly whisk sugar, egg yolks and orange zest.

Lightly whisk in cream, cinnamon and juice. (Lightly whisk so bubbles will not remain on surface of custard when it cooks.)

Divide mixture equally among prepared ramekins. Pour hot water into baking dish to reach halfway up sides of ramekins.

Bake for about 55 minutes or until custard is set around edges but jiggles slightly in center when gently shaken.

Remove from water bath and cool on rack. Chill for several hours before serving. (These may be made 1 or 2 days in advance.)

Optional: If desired, beat ½ cup whipping cream with 1 tablespoon powdered sugar. Spoon dollop of whipped cream on top of each custard just before serving.

Rice Pudding with Boysenberry Sauce

4 cups whole milk
¾ cup uncooked long-grain rice
⅓ cup sugar
1 large egg
1 cup boysenberry sauce

Heat milk in medium-heavy saucepan over medium heat. Stir in rice and bring to simmer.

Simmer uncovered, stirring occasionally, for 30 minutes, until rice is tender. Remove from heat.

In small bowl, whisk together sugar and egg. Quickly stir egg mixture into rice mixture.

Blend thoroughly and place back on medium heat. Simmer for 1 minute.

Remove from heat and spoon into 8 x 8-inch square baking pan.

Cool to room temperature, cover and chill until ready to serve. Chill at least 1 hour.

To serve, place portion of rice pudding on plate and spoon boysenberry sauce over each portion.

Tip: Boysenberry Sauce is also available in grocery stores or the recipe is on page 10.

Floating Islands

Also known as "snow eggs," this light classic dessert consists of "islands" of sweetened meringue poached in milk and floated in a custard sauce. It is delightfully simple to make.

3 eggs, separated
11 tablespoons sugar, divided
2 tablespoons flour
3 cups milk
1 teaspoon vanilla

Whisk egg yolks, 5 tablespoons sugar and flour in top of double boiler. Stir in milk.

Place double boiler over simmering water and cook until mixture coats back of spoon. Stir in vanilla.

Remove from heat and pour mixture into 2-quart baking dish.

To make meringue, beat egg whites and remaining 6 tablespoons sugar until stiff peaks form.

Drop by tablespoons onto cooked custard. Place under broiler and brown slightly. Chill before serving.

Almond Custard with Chocolate Sauce
"Simple-ly" delicious!

3 cups heavy whipping cream, divided
½ cup sugar
6 egg yolks
¼ teaspoon almond extract
3 (1 ounce) squares semi-sweet baking chocolate

Combine 2½ cups cream and sugar in medium saucepan and bring to boil over medium heat, stirring frequently.

Immediately remove from heat and cool to room temperature.

Heat oven to 350° and place 6 custard cups in 9 x 13-inch baking dish.

Whisk egg yolks and almond extract into cream mixture, just until blended. (Try not to make frothy.)

Ladle cream mixture into custard cups, filling each evenly.

Place baking dish in oven and make water bath by adding enough hot water to baking dish to bring water level halfway up sides of custard cups.

Bake for 40 to 45 minutes until centers are set, but loose and knife inserted in center comes out clean.

Remove from oven and place custard cups on cooling rack to cool. Cover and chill until ready to serve.

To serve, turn custard out of custard dish onto plate. Loosen custard first by running sharp knife around edges. Drizzle chocolate sauce over top of each custard before serving.

(continued on next page)

(continued)

Chocolate Sauce

Combine remaining ½ cup whipping cream and chocolate in small saucepan.

Cook over low heat, stirring constantly, until chocolate melts and mixture is smooth and slightly thick.

Remove from heat and cool to room temperature. Put in covered container and chill until ready to use.

Makes about ¾ cup.

Optional: Sprinkle toasted, slivered almonds on top.

Blancmange

2 cups half-and-half cream, divided
3 tablespoons cornstarch
⅓ cup sugar
½ teaspoon almond extract

Place 1½ cups cream in top of double boiler and heat until bubbles appear around edges.

In small bowl, combine cornstarch and sugar with remaining ½ cup cream. Stir until smooth.

Add to cream in top of double boiler and cook over simmering water for 10 minutes or until thick and smooth, stirring frequently.

Cover and cook for an additional 15 minutes, stirring occasionally.

Remove from heat and beat in almond extract. Divide among 4 (4-ounce) ramekins. Chill well before serving.

Maple Creme Brulee

4 egg yolks
½ cup maple syrup
2½ cups half-and-half
2½ teaspoons sugar

Preheat oven to 350°.

In medium bowl, whisk egg yolks with maple syrup and half-and-half.

Place 6 creme brulee dishes or custard cups in large baking dish.

Divide egg yolk mixture among custard cups and place on oven rack.

Pour enough hot water into large baking dish to come halfway up sides of cups.

Bake for 40 to 45 minutes or until custard is set and knife inserted in middle comes out clean.

Remove from water bath and cool on rack. Chill.

When ready to serve, sprinkle about 1 teaspoon sugar evenly over surface of each and place under broiler.

Broil until sugar melts slightly and forms a crisp coating.

Cool again or chill for a few minutes and serve.

Peach Creme Brulee

2 cups half-and-half
5 egg yolks, slightly beaten
⅓ cup plus ¼ cup sugar
1 teaspoon vanilla
1 (14 ounce) can peach halves in syrup, drained

Heat half-and-half in heavy saucepan over medium heat until it starts to bubble. Remove from heat and set aside.

Combine egg yolks, ⅓ cup sugar and vanilla and whisk to blend.

Slowly whisk in hot cream until just combined. Do not make it frothy or bubbles will remain when it cools.

Preheat oven to 325°.

Place 6 creme brulee dishes or custard cups in 9 x 13-inch baking dish.

Place layer of peach slices in bottom of each dish. (There may be peaches leftover.)

Pour custard over peaches. The peaches will rise a little and may appear on the surface.

Place baking pan on oven rack. Make water bath by carefully pouring enough hot water into baking pan to come halfway up sides of dishes. (This helps custard cook evenly.)

Bake for 34 to 40 minutes until knife inserted in center comes out clean.

(continued on next page)

(continued)

Remove custard dishes from baking dish and cool on wire rack. Cover and chill at least 1 hour.

When ready to serve, sprinkle remaining ¼ cup sugar evenly over surface of each cup. Place custard dishes under broiler until sugar melts slightly and forms a crisp coating. (Be careful not to burn.)

Chill again for few minutes and serve.

Mint Chocolate Creme Anglaise

1 cup heavy whipping cream
2 cups whole milk
5 egg yolks
6 tablespoons sugar
2 (3.5 ounce) premium mint chocolate bars, crumbled

Combine cream and milk in medium saucepan and heat just until bubbles appear around edges.

While milk mixture is heating, whisk egg yolks and sugar in medium bowl.

Slowly add hot milk mixture to egg yolks, whisking vigorously, until mixture blends

Pour mixture into top of double boiler and cook over very low heat until mixture thickens, about 5 minutes, and coats back of spoon. (It's ready when a finger run across spoon leaves a trail.) Be careful not to overheat mixture or it will curdle.

Remove from heat and add chocolate. Whisk until chocolate melts and mixture is smooth.

Strain into a bowl to remove few small solids that may have formed as it cooked. Cool to room temperature, cover and chill for several hours before serving.

To serve, spoon into 6 to 8 dessert glasses. Top each with dollop of whipped cream and additional grated chocolate.

Chocolate Cream

12 (1 ounce) squares semi-sweet baking chocolate
4 tablespoons water
2 teaspoons vanilla
1½ cups heavy whipping cream

In small saucepan, melt chocolate in 4 tablespoons water. Stir constantly until mixture is smooth and all chocolate melts.

Stir in vanilla. Remove from heat and set aside to cool.

Beat whipping cream until stiff peaks form.

Fold chocolate mixture into whipped cream until mixture is thoroughly blended and evenly colored. Chill before serving.

Fill cream puff shells using pastry bag or tight plastic bag with corner cut off.

Amaretto Pot de Creme au Chocolate

Pot de Creme, pronounced "poh duh KREHM," is a French word meaning "pot of cream". This dessert is a creamy rich, chocolate-flavored custard prepared and served in tiny pot-shaped cups or custard cups. Although traditionally flavored with vanilla, pot de creme has many variations. Amaretto gives this chocolate version a lovely almond flavor.

4 (1 ounce) squares semi-sweet chocolate
1½ cups light cream
6 egg yolks, slightly beaten
2 tablespoons amaretto liqueur

Place chocolate and cream in top of double boiler and cook over simmering water until chocolate melts. Stir until mixture is smooth.

Spoon some of hot chocolate mixture into egg yolks and stir to blend.

Add egg yolk mixture to chocolate mixture in double boiler.

Add amaretto and continue cooking, stirring constantly, until mixture thickens, about 5 or 6 minutes.

Spoon into 8 pot de creme cups or 4 (6 ounce) custard cups and cool. Chill at least 1 hour and serve.

Tip: This is great served with dollop of whipped cream.

Chocolate Creme Brulee

2 cups half-and-half
5 egg yolks, slightly beaten
⅓ cup packed brown sugar plus ⅓ cup brown sugar, not packed
1 teaspoon vanilla
3 (1 ounce) squares semi-sweet chocolate, melted, cooled

In medium saucepan over medium heat, bring half-and-half to simmer or low boil. Immediately remove from heat and set aside.

In medium bowl, whisk together egg yolks, ⅓ cup brown sugar and vanilla.

Whisk in chocolate until mixture blends.

Heat oven to 325°.

Place custard cups or creme brulee dishes in 9 x 13-baking dish. Pour mixture into custard cups or creme brulee dishes.

Place baking dish on oven rack. Make water bath by pouring enough hot water into baking dish to come halfway up sides of custard cups.

Bake for 35 to 40 minutes until knife inserted in center of custard comes out clean.

Remove from oven and take custard cups out of water bath. Place on cooling rack.

When cool, chill until almost ready to serve. When ready to serve, sprinkle remaining brown sugar evenly over surface of each custard and place dishes under broiler.

Broil until sugar melts slightly and forms crisp coating.

Chill and serve.

Raspberry Crowned Chocolate Mousse in Ladyfinger Ring

3 (6 ounce) containers fresh raspberries, divided
1 cup sugar
2 (4 ounce) bars premium semi-sweet chocolate
2 cups heavy whipping cream
3 (3 ounce) packages ladyfingers

Puree or mash 12 ounces raspberries using a potato masher and strain juice into small, heavy saucepan.

Discard solids. Set aside 1 container of raspberries for garnish.

To make raspberry sauce, add sugar to juice in saucepan and stir over medium heat until sugar dissolves and mixture simmers.

Cook for 15 minutes, stirring occasionally, until mixture thickens.

Remove from heat and set aside to cool or chill until ready to use. (Raspberry sauce should be very thick, almost like a jelly, when cool. It will be more fluid when warm.)

To make chocolate mousse, melt chocolate in small, heavy saucepan over very low heat, stirring until smooth.

Set aside and cool to room temperature.

In bowl, beat whipping cream until stiff peaks form. Fold cooled chocolate into cream until well blended.

Split ladyfingers. Place as many as necessary in single layer in bottom of 9-inch springform pan to cover completely.

(continued on next page)

(continued)

Place additional ladyfingers on end touching sides of springform pan to form a ring. (It will look like a crown.)

Spread half mousse mixture evenly over ladyfingers in bottom of pan.

Place remaining ladyfingers on top of mousse, as evenly as possible, covering mousse completely.

Pour half or a little more raspberry syrup evenly over ladyfingers.

Place remaining mousse on top and smooth over as much as possible.

Pour remaining raspberry syrup evenly over top, starting from middle and working toward edges. (It doesn't need to extend all the way to the edge.)

Arrange remaining raspberries attractively on top. Cover and chill for about 6 hours or overnight to set.

Options: For additional flavor, add 2 to 3 tablespoons raspberry liqueur (chambord) to whipping cream before beating. Also, if you're ambitious, whip up a little extra cream (about ½ cup) and pipe rosettes around edges of top and place a raspberry on each.

Mousse

Mousse is a French term meaning "froth" or "foam". This light, but rich dish may be sweet or savory, hot or cold. Cold dessert mousses are usually made with fruit puree or a flavoring such as chocolate. Whipped cream or beaten egg whites gives them the fluffiness.

Creamy Chocolate Mousse

What a dreamy delight!
This thick, velvety smooth mousse is a favorite every time.

1 (12 ounce) bag semi-sweet chocolate chips
3 cups heavy whipping cream, divided
2 tablespoons orange liqueur
⅓ cup powdered sugar

Combine chocolate chips and 1 cup whipping cream in heavy, medium saucepan.

Cook over low to medium heat, stirring constantly, until chocolate melts and mixture is smooth.

Stir in orange liqueur. Set aside and cool to room temperature.

In large bowl, beat remaining 2 cups whipping cream and powdered sugar until stiff peaks form.

Gently fold in chocolate mixture until well blended and evenly colored.

Spoon into 8 dessert cups. Cover and chill for several hours or until ready to serve.

Optional: For a really nice finish, garnish each dessert with a pretty cookie such as a pirouette to give it a little extra flair. Top with dollop of whipped cream and place a chocolate-dipped, candied orange peel on top.

Sunny Citrus Mango Mousse

This lovely orange-colored mousse has a delicate citrus flavor. Because it is refreshing and cool, but not overly sweet, it makes a terrific summertime dessert.

2 oranges
⅓ cup plus ¼ cup cold water
1 cup sugar
1 (.25 ounce) packet unflavored gelatin
3 cups heavy whipping cream
1 very ripe mango, peeled, pureed

Squeeze juice from 2 oranges to equal ½ cup. Add water if necessary. Grate peel of oranges for zest.

Place juice and orange peel in small saucepan and cook over low heat. Stir in ⅓ cup water and sugar.

Cook and stir until sugar dissolves and remove from heat.

Stir gelatin into ¼ cup cold water until dissolved. Add to orange mixture and stir to blend. Set aside to cool.

Whip cream until soft peaks form. Fold in cooled orange-gelatin mixture until well blended and gently fold in pureed mango.

Place mousse mixture in lightly greased mold and chill several hours until firm. Turn mold onto serving plate just before serving.

Tip: Any decorative mold will make this a beautiful dish. (I use a small bundt cake pan with has decorative sides.) To oil mold, place ½ teaspoonful oil into mold and spread with paper towel to coat all indentations of mold.

Lemon Curd Mousse with Blackberry Sauce

These light, airy lemon-flavored mousse parfaits are enhanced by a layer of sweet lemon curd and tangy blackberry sauce.

1 (6 ounce) container blackberries
½ cup water
½ cup sugar
2 cups (1 pint) heavy whipping cream
1¾ cups lemon curd, divided

Wash blackberries and place in heavy medium saucepan with water and sugar.

Bring to boil over medium high heat and stir to dissolve sugar.

Reduce heat to simmer and cook for 10 minutes, crushing berries with a potato masher or back of spoon to release juices.

Strain mixture into container and cool. Discard solids and chill juice until ready to use.

Beat whipping cream until stiff peaks form. Remove ¾ cup for garnish.

Fold 1 cup lemon curd into remaining cream until well mixed. The remaining ¾ cup lemon curd will be used as 1 layer in parfaits.

To assemble parfaits, spoon a little blackberry sauce into bottom of 6 (6-8 ounce) dessert cups. (You will not use all the sauce.)

Divide half of mousse mixture between cups and spoon it over blackberry sauce.

Spoon some of reserved ¾ cup lemon curd on top of mousse. Spoon remaining half of mousse over lemon curd.

(continued on next page)

(continued)

Top with dollop of reserved whipped cream and serve.

Tip: Buy a few extra blackberries to use as garnish. Just place 2 or 3 on top of whipped cream to top off the dessert. Omit blackberry sauce and serve parfaits without it. They taste are delightful just by themselves!

Lemon Curd

4 lemons
1 tablespoon lemon zest
3 tablespoons butter
½ cup sugar
1 large egg, plus 1 large egg yolk

Squeeze ⅓ cup juice from lemons and grate peel for zest.

Place lemon juice, lemon zest, butter and sugar in top of double boiler over gently simmering water.

Stir until butter melts and sugar dissolves. Water must be hot enough to melt butter and dissolve sugar, but not too hot or eggs will cook when you add them in the next step.

Beat eggs in a separate bowl and slowly add to lemon mixture in pan. Stir quickly and thoroughly as you add them.

Pour mixture into small, heavy saucepan and place over low heat. Cook and stir frequently until mixture thickens, about 5 or 6 minutes. (It should coat the back of a spoon and elave a trail when you run your finger through it.)

Remove from heat and cool. Cover and chill.

Yields 1 cup.

Fresh Strawberry Mousse

When red, ripe strawberries are in season,
they make this light, summery dessert a showpiece.

¼ cup cold water
1 (.25 ounce) packet unflavored gelatin
2 cups hulled, sliced strawberries plus a few whole ones
¼ cup plus 3 tablespoons sugar
1 cup heavy whipping cream

Pour water in small saucepan and sprinkle gelatin over water.

Stir over low heat until gelatin dissolves, about 1 minute. Remove from heat.

Set aside whole strawberries for garnish.

Put sliced strawberries, ¼ cup sugar and gelatin mixture in blender or food processor and puree.

Pour mixture into bowl and chill for 1 hour to thicken.

Put remaining 3 tablespoons sugar and whipping cream in bowl and beat on high speed until soft peaks form.

Fold in strawberry mixture, a little at a time, until mousse is well blended.

Garnish with fresh strawberries. Chill until ready to serve.

Cappuccino Mousse

1 (14 ounce) can sweetened condensed milk
⅓ cup cocoa
3 tablespoons margarine
2 teaspoons powdered instant coffee
2 cups cold whipping cream

Dissolve instant coffee in 2 teaspoons water.

Combine condensed milk, cocoa, butter and coffee in saucepan.

Cook over low heat, stirring constantly, until butter melts and mixture is smooth.

Remove from heat and cool.

In large bowl beat whipping cream until stiff. Gradually fold chocolate mixture into cream.

Spoon into dessert dishes.

Chill until set.

Souffle

Souffle is a spongy dish made from a sweet or savory mixture, often using milk or cheese, and lightened by stiffly beaten egg whites or whipped cream. Dessert souffles may be baked, chilled or frozen and are most often flavored with fruit purees, chocolate, lemon or liqueurs.

The word "souffle" is derived from the French verb "to blow". This dish is light and airy as a result of being leavened by beaten egg whites and heat. Souffles should be served immediately from the oven, before they have any chance to deflate. Once removed from the oven, the hot air trapped in the souffle begins to escape causing the mixture to deflate.

Chocolate Souffles

With their crowns rising about 2 inches from the rim of baking cups, these individual souffles look very striking. Served warm from the oven, they just melt in your mouth.

5 (1 ounce) squares semi-sweet chocolate
5 tablespoons butter
½ cup sugar
2 eggs plus 2 egg yolks
½ cup flour

Preheat oven to 400°.

Grease and flour 5 (6 ounce) ramekins.

In top of double boiler or in small, heavy saucepan, melt chocolate in butter over low heat. Stir frequently until mixture is smooth and all chocolate melts. Remove from heat and cool to lukewarm.

In separate bowl, combine sugar with eggs and egg yolks.

Beat on high speed for about 6 minutes until mixture is very thick and falls in ribbons when beaters are lifted.

Sprinkle flour over egg mixture and gently fold.

Gradually add chocolate mixture and gently fold until all chocolate is blended and mixture is evenly colored.

Place prepared ramekins on baking sheet and fill with batter.

Bake for 17 to 18 minutes until souffles puff on top. Serve immediately.

Tip: Although these should be served immediately after baking, they can be prepared in advance, put in baking dishes, covered and baked 20 minutes before serving. They may be chilled up to 1 day before baking.

Orange Souffles

5 eggs, separated, divided
5 tablespoons plus 5 teaspoons sugar, divided
¼ cup orange juice, plus 1 teaspoon orange zest
1 tablespoon orange liqueur
2 tablespoons plus 1 teaspoon flour

Preheat oven to 350°.

Prepare 5 (6 ounce) souffle dishes by lightly greasing with butter and dusting with 1 teaspoon sugar for each dish. Set aside.

In medium bowl, beat 3 egg yolks until thick and pale about 5 minutes.

Add 2 tablespoons sugar, orange juice, zest, orange liqueur and flour. Beat again until well mixed and set aside.

In small bowl, beat 5 egg whites until thick and foamy. Gradually add 3 tablespoons sugar and continue to beat until whites are glossy and stiff peaks form.

Gently fold egg white mixture into egg yolk mixture in several additions until well blended.

Spoon mixture into prepared dishes and bake for 20 minutes. Serve immediately.

Chilled Pumpkin Souffle

2½ cups heavy whipping cream, divided
1 (30 ounce) can pumpkin pie filling, divided
2 (.25 ounce) packets unflavored gelatin
¼ cup light rum
½ teaspoon pumpkin pie spice

Make foil collar for 1½-quart souffle dish by taking aluminum foil 4-inches longer than circumference of dish. Fold into thirds lengthwise and wrap around outside of dish leaving 2-inch collar extending above sides of dish. Tape overlapping edges to fasten.

In large bowl, beat 2 cups whipping cream until soft peaks form. Set aside.

Place ½ pumpkin pie filling and gelatin in medium saucepan over low heat.

Stir until gelatin dissolves about 4 minutes. Remove from heat.

Put remaining pumpkin pie filling in large bowl and stir in hot gelatin mixture, rum and pumpkin pie spice. Gently fold whipped cream into pumpkin mixture.

Pour pumpkin mixture into souffle dish. Cover with plastic wrap and chill for several hours.

To serve, remove foil collar. Beat remaining ½ cup whipped cream and spread on top.

Tip: The souffle will keep in the refrigerator for 2 days, so you may make this dish in advance.

Creamy Peach Parfait Topped With Almonds

1 (3 ounce) package cream cheese, softened
1 (14 ounce) can sweetened condensed milk
⅓ cup lemon juice
1 (20 ounce) can peach pie filling
¼ cup sliced almonds, toasted

In medium bowl, beat cream cheese until light and fluffy.

Gradually stir in sweetened condensed milk and lemon juice and blend well.

Into each parfait glass, spoon about 1 tablespoon cheese mixture and about 2 tablespoons pie filling. Repeat layering.

Top with dollop of cheese mixture and sliced, toasted almonds.

Banana Crunch Parfaits

Here's a 5-minute recipe for some very attractive and tasty parfaits. The parfaits combine crunchy toffee and buttery shortbread with creamy pudding and bananas. Top all that off with whipped cream and toffee and it is not bad for 5-minutes!

½ cup crushed shortbread cookies
6 (3.5 ounce) containers vanilla pudding, divided
1½ bananas
½ cup crushed chocolate-covered toffee candy bar, divided
1 cup frozen whipped topping, thawed or whipped cream

Divide shortbread cookie crumbs evenly in bottom of 6 dessert cups.

Using 3 pudding containers, spoon half a container of vanilla pudding over crumbs in each of cups.

Cut bananas in thick slices and divide them evenly on top of vanilla pudding.

Sprinkle toffee pieces over bananas, but reserve a few teaspoonfuls for garnish.

Use remaining 3 pudding containers to place half a container of pudding over toffee.

Divide whipped topping among cups and place dollop in center of pudding in each cup.

Sprinkle reserved toffee over whipped topping for garnish. Keep chilled until ready to serve.

White Chocolate-Mocha Mousse Parfaits

1 cup milk chocolate chips
3 cups heavy whipping cream, divided
1 cup white chocolate chips
1 tablespoon instant coffee powder
⅓ cup powdered sugar

In small saucepan, combine milk chocolate chips, ½ cup whipping cream and instant coffee.

Cook over low to medium heat, stirring constantly, until chocolate melts and mixture is smooth. Set aside.

Do the same with white chocolate chips and ½ cup whipping cream. Set aside. Let both mixtures cool to room temperature.

In large bowl, beat remaining 2 cups whipping cream and powdered sugar until stiff peaks form.

Divide in half and gently fold half into chocolate mixture until well blended and evenly colored. Fold other half into white chocolate mixture until well blended.

Divide half white chocolate mixture among 6 or 8 dessert cups. Top with half chocolate mixture divided evenly among cups.

Repeat layers with white chocolate and chocolate mousse. Each cup will have 4 alternating layers of mousse.

Optional: For a special finish, top each one off with dollop of whipped cream and a few chocolate-coated coffee beans as garnish.

Lemon-Raspberry Parfaits
What a quick and easy, 5-minute recipe!

1 cup whipping cream, chilled
⅓ cup lowfat lemon-flavored yogurt
⅓ cup sugar
2 bananas
1 (12 ounce or smaller) bag frozen, sweetened raspberries or 1 pint fresh raspberries

In mixing bow, beat whipping cream with yogurt and sugar until soft peaks form.

Divide half of mixture among 4 dessert cups.

Slice bananas and arrange layer on top of whipped cream mixture in each cup.

Top with remaining cream mixture, divided equally among cups.

Sprinkle raspberries over surface of each. Chill until ready to serve.

Blueberry and Pudding Parfaits

2 cups (1 pint) fresh blueberries
½ cup water
½ cup sugar
1 tablespoon cornstarch
1 (22 ounce) container vanilla pudding

Reserve 6 blueberries for garnish and set aside.

Place remaining blueberries in medium saucepan with water. Bring to simmer and cook covered over medium heat for 12 to 15 minutes or until blueberries are soft.

Remove from heat and remove half blueberries. Mash remaining blueberries with potato masher or back of spoon to release all juice.

Strain and squeeze out as much juice as possible and discard pulp.

Place blueberries and blueberry juice back into saucepan and add sugar.

Mix cornstarch with 1 tablespoon cool water to make a paste and stir into blueberry-sugar mixture.

Bring to simmer again and cook over low heat until mixture thickens, about 4 to 6 minutes. Stir carefully to avoid crushing whole blueberries.

Remove from heat and cool to room temperature.

Divide half pudding among 6 small or 4 large dessert cups. Place tablespoonful blueberry sauce over pudding in each cup.

Divide remaining pudding among dessert cups, spreading it carefully over blueberry sauce. Cover with remaining blueberry sauce.

Optional: Top with whipped cream and garnish with a fresh, whole blueberry.

Pies

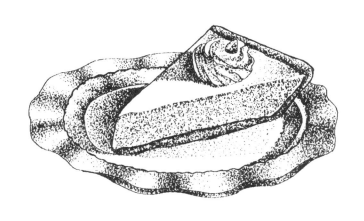

Strawberry-Cream Cheese Pie

1 (10 ounce) package frozen sweetened strawberries, thawed
2 (8 ounce) packages cream cheese, softened
⅔ cup powdered sugar
1 (8 ounce) carton whipped topping
1 (6 ounce) prepared chocolate crumb crust

Drain strawberries and reserve ¼ cup liquid.

In mixing bowl, combine cream cheese, reserved liquid, strawberries and sugar. Mix well.

Fold in whipped topping. Spoon into crust.

Chill overnight.

Garnish with fresh strawberries.

Strawberry Fluff Pie

32 marshmallows
½ cup milk
¾ cup sliced strawberries, divided
1 (8 ounce) carton frozen whipped topping, thawed
1 (9 inch) pie shell, baked

Combine marshmallows and milk in medium saucepan over medium heat.

Cook and stir until marshmallows melt. Remove from heat and cool.

Fold in ½ cup strawberries and frozen whipped topping. Pour into pie crust.

Arrange remaining strawberry slices on top and chill before serving.

Cool Strawberry Pie

This recipe makes enough for two pies. The strawberry-gelatin mixture is refreshing and not overly sweet. Freeze the extra one or give it away.

1 (16 ounce) bag frozen, unsweetened strawberries, thawed
1 (6 ounce) package dry strawberry gelatin
1 cup boiling water plus 1 cup cold water
1½ cups heavy whipping cream, divided
2 (6 ounce) graham cracker pie crusts

Puree strawberries in blender or food processor.

Place gelatin in large bowl. Pour boiling water into gelatin and stir until gelatin dissolves.

Stir in cold water and strawberry puree. Chill until it thickens slightly, about 1 hour.

Beat whipping cream until peaks form. Chill until ready to serve.

Beat gelatin mixture on high speed for 2 minutes, until mixture is frothy. Fold in ⅔ whipped cream and reserve ⅓ for garnish.

Spoon into pie crusts. Chill several hours until firm. Garnish with remaining whipped cream.

Snappy Strawberry Pie

This 5 minute, easy-to-make pie combines sweet and tart flavors. For a really great presentation, add some sliced kiwi to the top with strawberries. The bright colors really stand out and give it a festive look.

1 (14 ounce) can sweetened condensed milk
1-2 lemons
4 ounces frozen whipped topping, thawed
1 (6 ounce) shortbread crust
1 pint strawberries, hulled, halved

Squeeze lemons to get ¼ cup lemon juice.

In medium bowl, combine sweetened condensed mild with lemon juice and whisk until well blended.

Gently fold in whipped topping.

Pour mixture into prepared pie crust.

Arrange strawberry halves in attractive design on top. Keep chilled until ready to serve.

Strawberry-Strawberry Pie

2 pints fresh strawberries
1¼ cups sugar
3 tablespoons cornstarch
1 (9 inch) graham cracker pie crust
1 (8 ounce) carton whipping cream, whipped

Crush 1 pint strawberries, add sugar, cornstarch and a dash of salt.

Cook on low heat until thick and clear. Cool.

Place reserved pint of strawberries in pie shell and cover with cooked mixture.

Top with whipped topping. Chill.

Strawberry-Yogurt Pie

**1 (12 ounce) carton frozen whipped topping
1 (1 pint) carton strawberry yogurt
½ cup sliced strawberries
1 (6 ounce) graham cracker crust**

Combine whipped topping and yogurt and blend well.

Fold in strawberries.

Pour mixture into pie crust and freeze until firm.

Very Merry Berry Pie

**1 (6 ounce) package strawberry gelatin
1 cup whole berry cranberry sauce
½ cup cranberry juice cocktail
1 (8 ounce) carton whipped topping
1 (9 inch) baked pie shell**

Dissolve gelatin in 1 cup boiling water.

Add cranberry sauce and juice. Chill until it begins to thicken.

Fold in whipped topping and chill again until mixture will mound.

Pour into pie shell.

Chill several hours before serving.

Old-Fashioned Cherry Pie

4 cups pitted, red tart cherries
1¼ cup sugar
¼ cup flour
¼ teaspoon cinnamon
2 tablespoons butter

Preheat oven to 425°.

Prepare crust for 1 (9 inch) pie pan with 2 pie crusts.

In large bowl, lightly stir peaches and sugar together.

Stir in flour and lemon juice. Spoon into pie pan with bottom crust.

Dot with butter and place top crust over pie filling.

Fold edges of top crust under edges of bottom crust to seal. Flute edges with fingers.

Cut several slit in top crust.

Bake for 15 minutes and remove pie from oven. Cover edges of pie crust with foil to keep them from burning.

Return to oven and bake for 20 to 25 minutes or until pie is bubbly and crust is golden brown.

Old-Fashioned Peach Pie

5 cups peeled, sliced fresh peaches
¾ cup sugar
⅓ cup flour
1 tablespoon lemon juice
2 tablespoons butter

Preheat oven to 425°.

Prepare crust for 1 (9 inch) pie pan with 2 pie crusts.

In large bowl, lightly stir peaches and sugar together. (If peaches are tart, add a little more sugar.)

Stir in flour and lemon juice. Spoon into pie pan with bottom crust.

Dot with butter and place top crust over pie filling.

Fold edges of top crust under edges of bottom crust to seal. Flute edges with fingers.

Cut several slit in top crust.

Bake for 15 minutes and remove pie from oven. Cover edges of pie crust with foil to keep them from burning.

Return to oven and bake for 15 to 20 minutes or until pie is bubbly and crust is light, golden brown.

Old-Fashioned Blueberry Pie

4 cups fresh blueberries
¾ cup sugar
¼ cup flour
2 tablespoons lemon juice
2 tablespoons butter

Preheat oven to 425°.

Prepare crust for 1 (9 inch) pie pan with 2 pie crusts.

In large bowl, lightly stir blueberries and sugar together. (If blueberries are tart, add a little more sugar.)

Stir in flour and lemon juice. Spoon into pie pan with bottom crust.

Dot with butter and place top crust over pie filling.

Fold edges of top crust under edges of bottom crust to seal. Flute edges with fingers.

Cut several slit in top crust.

Bake for 15 minutes and remove pie from oven. Cover edges of pie crust with foil to keep them from burning.

Return to oven and bake for 30 to 40 minutes or until pie is bubbly and crust is golden brown.

Creamy Lemon Pie

1 (8 ounce) package cream cheese, softened
1 (14 ounce) can sweetened condensed milk
¼ cup lemon juice
1 (20 ounce) can lemon pie filling
1 (9 inch) graham cracker pie crust

In mixing bowl, cream cheese until creamy.

Add sweetened condensed milk and lemon juice.

Beat until mixture is very creamy.

Fold in lemon pie filling and stir well.

Pour into pie curst.

Chill several hours before serving.

Banana-Cream Cheese Pie

1 (8 ounce) package cream cheese, softened
1 (14 ounce) can sweetened condensed milk
⅓ cup fresh lemon juice
4 bananas
1 (9 inch) chocolate pie crust

In large bowl beat cream cheese until light and fluffy.

Gradually beat in sweetened condensed milk until mixture is smooth.

Slice bananas and dip banana slices in lemon juice.

Drain and use half slices to line crust. Reserve other half for topping.

Stir remaining lemon juice into cream cheese filling mixture.

Pour filling over bananas. Arrange remaining banana slices on top of filling.

Cover and chill for several hours to set.

Chocolate-Coconut Pie

1½ cups flaked coconut
1½ cups chopped pecans
1 (12 ounce) package chocolate chips
1 (6 ounce) prepared chocolate crust
1 (14 ounce) can sweetened condensed milk

Preheat oven at 350°.

Combine coconut, pecans and chocolate chips. Sprinkle mixture over crust.

Spoon sweetened condensed milk evenly over coconut mixture.

Bake for 25 to 30 minutes. Cool before serving.

Solo Chocolate Pies

**1 (4 serving) package vanilla cook & serve
pudding and pie filling mix***
**1 cup plus ¼ cup miniature, semi-sweet chocolate chips, divided
1 (4 ounce) package (6 count) miniature graham cracker crusts
Whipped topping**

Prepare pudding and pie filling mix according to package directions. Remove from heat.

Immediately add 1 cup chocolate chips and stir until chips melt.

Set aside to cool, about 5 minutes, and stir occasionally.

Pour pie filling into individual crusts and cover with plastic wrap. Chill several hours until firm.

When ready to serve, place a dollop of whipped cream on each individual pie and sprinkle with remaining chocolate chips.

Tip: Do not use instant pudding mix.

Chilled Chocolate Mocha Pie

2 tablespoons butter
1 (12 ounce) package semi-sweet or milk chocolate chips
2½ cups crisped rice cereal
1 quart coffee ice cream, softened
3½-4 ounces shaved chocolate

Melt butter and chocolate chips in top of double boiler set over simmering water and stir until mixture is smooth.

Remove from heat and stir in crisped rice.

Spread mixture evenly in bottom of 9-inch pie dish and chill until set.

Spread ice cream in prepared crust and freeze for several hours.

Remove from freezer and garnish with shaved chocolate. Let pie sit at room temperature for a few minutes before serving.

Creme de Menthe Pie

24 large marshmallows
4 tablespoons milk
4 tablespoons green creme de menthe
½ pint heavy whipping cream, whipped
1 (6 ounce) prepared chocolate pie crust

Melt marshmallows with milk in top of double boiler set over simmering water. Stir until mixture is smooth. Remove from heat and cool.

Add creme de menthe and fold whipped cream into mixture.

Pour into crust and chill overnight.

Optional: Before serving, sprinkle grated chocolate over top of pie.

Creme de menthe is a sweet, peppermint-flavored liqueur that comes in both colorless and green varieties.

Irish Cream Delight

½ cup milk
32 large marshmallows
⅓ cup Irish cream liqueur
1½ cups heavy whipping cream
1 (6 ounce) prepared chocolate cookie pie crust

Place milk and marshmallows in large saucepan over low heat. Stir constantly until marshmallows melt.

Remove mixture from pan and chill about 30 minutes, stirring occasionally. Mixture is ready if it mounds slightly when dropped from spoon.

Slowly add liqueur to marshmallow mixture and stir well after each addition.

While mixture is chilling, beat whipping cream in medium bowl until stiff peaks form. Cover and chill.

Gently fold marshmallow mixture into cream. Pour into pie crust.

Cover and chill 3 to 4 hours until pie is set.

Sweet Potato Pie

1 (15 ounce) can sweet potatoes, drained, mashed
3 eggs
1 cup sugar
1 tablespoon butter, melted
1 (9 inch) pie crust, unbaked

Preheat oven to 350°.

In large bowl combine sweet potatoes, eggs, sugar and butter. Beat until well blended.

Pour into unbaked pie shell. Bake until brown, about 1 hour.

If desired, remove pie from oven about 5 minutes early and top with ½ cup pecans and 1 cup miniature marshmallows.

Return to oven until marshmallows are lightly browned.

Toffee-Caramel Pie

2 (14 ounce) cans sweetened condensed milk
1 (6 ounce) prepared graham cracker crust
2 cups whipping cream
½ cup firmly packed brown sugar
1 (1.4 ounce) chocolate-covered toffee candy bar, crushed

Preheat oven at 425°.

Pour sweetened condensed milk into 11 x 7-inch baking dish and cover with aluminum foil.

Create water bath by placing baking dish inside 13 x 9-inch baking dish and add enough hot water to the larger dish to come up the sides 1 inch.

Bake for 1 hour 20 minutes until condensed milk is caramel colored and thick. If needed add water to large baking dish during baking as it evaporates.

Remove smaller dish from larger dish, pour caramelized milk into prepared crust and cool.

Combine whipping cream and brown sugar in small bowl and beat until soft peaks form.

Spread whipped cream over caramel filling and sprinkle crushed toffee over top.

Old-Fashioned Pecan Pie

This vintage recipe is more than 75 years old and was passed down through mothers and daughters.

3 eggs, beaten
1 cup sugar
1 cup white corn syrup
1 cup pecans
1 teaspoon vanilla
1 (9 inch) unbaked pie crust

Preheat oven to 300°.

Beat eggs and sugar until lemon colored. Add corn syrup, pecans and vanilla and mix well.

Pour into unbaked pie crust. Bake for 1 hour or until center of pie is set.

FRANCES PARHAM

Creamy Pecan Pie

1½ cups light corn syrup
1 (3 ounce) package vanilla instant pudding
3 eggs
5⅓ tablespoons (⅓ stick) margarine, melted
2 cups pecan halves
1 (9 inch deep dish) unbaked pie crust

Combine corn syrup, vanilla pudding, eggs and margarine and stir well. Fold in pecans.

Pour into unbaked deep dish pie crust. Cover pie crust edges with strips of foil to prevent excessive browning.

Bake at 350° for 35 to 40 minutes or until center of pie is set.

Easy, Breezy Lemonade Pie

6 ounces frozen lemonade concentrate, thawed
1 quart vanilla ice cream, softened
1 (8 ounce) can crushed pineapple, drained
1 (4 ounce) container whipped topping
1 (9 ounce) prepared graham cracker pie crust

Mix together lemonade concentrate, ice cream an pineapple until well blended.

Fold in whipped topping.

Pour into prepared pie crust.

Freeze at least 4 hours or overnight before serving.

Optional: Garnish with lemon slices.

Easy Graham Cracker Crust

24 graham cracker squares, crushed
⅓ cup butter, melted
3 tablespoons sugar

Preheat oven to 350°.

Mix graham cracker crumbs with butter and sugar.

Press into 9-inch pie pan so bottom and sides have the same thickness.

Bake 5 to 10 minutes until crust is light brown. Cool before filling.

Strawberry-Fruit Pizza

1 (18 ounce) package sugar cookie dough
1 (8 ounce) package cream cheese, softened
½ cup sugar
1 pint strawberries or raspberries
⅓ cup strawberry jelly for glaze

Preheat oven to 350°.

Spread cookie dough into ungreased pizza pan.

Bake for 10 to 15 minutes or until dough is lightly browned around edges and cooked in middle.

Remove from oven and cool.

Blend cream cheese and sugar until light and fluffy. Spread mixture over cooled crust.

Arrange strawberries on top.

Warm strawberry jelly and brush over strawberries with pastry brush.

Chill before serving.

Optional: Add other fruits for more colors and flavors.

Strawberry-Topped Cheesecake

Here is a quick way to turn a plain dessert into a sophisticated taste treat in 5 minutes! Take a prepared cheesecake, top it with glazed fresh fruit and serve it with a spiked sauce. You will have an impressive, delicious dessert in no time.

1 pint fresh strawberries
1 (8 or 10-inch) prepared plain cheesecake
½ cup strawberry preserves
1 tablespoon raspberry liqueur

Hull strawberries and cut in half. Arrange attractively on top of cheesecake.

Warm strawberry preserves in saucepan or microwave for 30 to 45 seconds on HIGH.

Stir and brush glaze onto strawberries with a pastry brush.

To make sauce, add raspberry liqueur to remaining strawberry preserves and stir well. Serve sauce over slices of cheesecake.

Mix strawberries and raspberries or use just raspberries.

Tip: Be sure to serve this right away because the strawberry juice will discolor the cheesecake.

Chocolate Cheesecake on Brownie Crust

1 (1 pound, 2 ounce) package ready-to-bake brownies
3 (8 ounce) packages cream cheese, softened
½ cup sugar
1 (8 ounce) carton frozen whipped topping, thawed
3 tablespoons semi-sweet chocolate, melted

Preheat oven at 350°.

Lightly grease bottom of 9 x 13-inch baking pan. Press brownie dough evenly into pan.

Bake for 20 minutes. Remove from oven to cool.

In large bowl, beat cream cheese and sugar until well mixed.

Beat whipped topping on low speed.

Remove one-third of cream cheese mixture and set aside. Stir chocolate into remaining two-thirds of mixture.

Spread chocolate-cheese mixture evenly over cooled brownie crust.

Carefully spread plain cream cheese mixture on top of chocolate. Chill until firm.

Optional: For an extra special touch, drizzle chocolate topping over each slice or grate some chocolate and arrange shavings on surface.

Crunchy Caramel-Topped Cheesecake

This is a terrific, 5-minute recipe.

**1 (6 or 8-inch) prepared cheesecake
1 (12 ounce) jar caramel topping or caramel sauce
3 chocolate-covered toffee bars, crushed**

Spread caramel topping over top of cheesecake. Sprinkle crushed toffee over caramel.

Cut and serve.

Tip: There's a great caramel sauce recipe on page 9.

Easy Cheesecake

**2 (8 ounce) packages cream cheese, softened
½ cup sugar
½ teaspoon vanilla
2 eggs
1 (9 inch) graham cracker pie crust**

In mixing bowl, beat together cream cheese, sugar, vanilla and eggs.

Pour into pie crust.

Bake at 350° for 40 minutes.

Chill and serve as is or top with any canned pie filling.

Apricot Cobbler

Wonderful served hot with a scoop of ice cream or whipped cream!

1 (20 ounce) can apricot pie filling
1 (20 ounce) can crushed pineapple, undrained
1 cup chopped pecans
1 (18 ounce) yellow cake mix
1 cup (2 sticks) butter, melted

In sprayed 9 x 13-inch baking dish, pour pie filling and spread out evenly.

Spoon pineapple and juice over pie filling.

Sprinkle pecans over pineapple. Sprinkle cake mix over pecans.

Drizzle melted butter over cake mix.

Bake at 375° for 40 minutes or until lightly brown and crunchy.

Serve hot or at room temperature.

Blueberry Hill Crunch

1 (20 ounce) can crushed pineapple, undrained
1 (18 ounce) package yellow cake mix
3 cups fresh or frozen blueberries
⅔ cup sugar
½ cup (1 stick) margarine, melted

Spread pineapple in buttered or sprayed 9 x 13-inch baking dish.

Sprinkle with cake mix, blueberries and sugar. Drizzle with margarine. (If you really want to make it good, add 1 cup chopped pecans.)

Bake at 350° for 45 minutes or until bubbly.

Express Fruit Cobbler

Use any kind of fruit pie filling to create this fast,
last-minute cobbler for a great dessert.

2 (20 ounce) cans blueberry pie filling
½ cup (1 stick) butter, softened
1 (18 ounce) box white cake mix
1 egg

In 9 x 13-inch baking pan, spread pie filling to cover bottom.

In large bowl cream butter to a smooth texture.

Add dry cake mix and egg and blend well. (Mixture will be very stiff.)

Spoon mixture over pie filling.

Bake at 350° for 40 minutes or until golden brown.

Cut into 3-inch squares.

Tip: Substitute peach pie filling, apple pie filling or any fruit filling you
want in this recipe.

Berry Blue Cobbler

½ cup (1 stick) margarine, melted
1 cup self-rising flour
1¾ cups sugar
1 cup milk
1 (21 ounce) can blueberry pie filling

Pour margarine in 9-inch baking pan.

Mix flour and sugar in bowl. Slowly pour milk in mixture and stir.

Pour flour, sugar and milk over margarine and spoon pie filling over batter.

Bake at 300° for 1 hour. Top with whipped cream to serve.

Lightning Fast Peach Cobbler

½ cup (1 stick) butter or margarine
1 (20 ounce) can sliced peaches, drained
1 cup milk
1 cup sugar
1 cup flour

Preheat oven to 350°.

Melt butter in 9 x 13-inch baking dish. Place peaches on butter.

In medium bowl, combine milk, sugar and flour.

Pour over peaches.

Bake for 1 hour.

Option: Sprinkle 1 teaspoon cinnamon over peaches before adding milk mixture.

Special Peach Crisp

4¾ cups peeled, sliced peaches
3 tablespoons lemon juice
1 cup flour
1¾ cups sugar
1 egg, beaten

Place peaches in 9-inch baking dish and sprinkle lemon juice over top.

Mix together flour, sugar, egg and dash of salt.

Spread mixture over top of peaches. Dot with a little margarine.

Bake at 375° until golden brown.

Strawberry Cobbler

1 (20 ounce) can strawberry pie filling
1 (20 ounce) can cherry pie filling
1 (18 ounce) package white cake mix
1 cup (2 sticks) margarine, melted
¾ cup package slivered almonds

Spread pie fillings in sprayed 9 x 13-inch baking pan.

Sprinkle cake mix over pie fillings.

Drizzle melted margarine over top and sprinkle almonds over top.

Bake at 350° for 55 minutes.

Top with whipped topping or scoop of ice cream.

Peachy-Amaretto Crunch

2 (21 ounce) cans peach pie filling
½ cup amaretto liqueur
1 (18.25 ounce) white cake mix
1 cup blanched, slivered almonds
½ (1 stick) cup butter or margarine

Preheat oven at 350°.

Spread pie filling evenly in bottom of greased 9 x 13-inch baking dish.

Pour amaretto over filling.

Sprinkle cake mix evenly over top of pie filling.

Sprinkle with slivered almonds.

Slice butter into ⅛-inch slices and place over surface of cake mixture.

Bake for 40 to 45 minutes, until top is browned.

Peach Crumb

1 (21 ounce) can peach pie filling
½ cup quick-cooking oats
½ cup flour
½ cup firmly packed brown sugar
¼ cup (½ stick) butter or margarine, melted

Preheat oven at 350°.

Pour peach pie filling in 8 x 8-inch baking dish.

In medium bowl, combine oats, flour and brown sugar.

Stir in butter until mixture is thoroughly blended.

Sprinkle mixture evenly over peach pie filling.

Bake for 40 to 45 minutes or until topping is brown.

Apple Crisp

5 cups peeled, cored, sliced apples
½ cup (1 stick) butter or margarine, melted
1 cup quick-cooking oats
½ cup firmly packed brown sugar
⅓ cup flour

Preheat over to 375°.

Place apple slices in 8 x 8-inch or 9 x 9-inch square baking pan.

Combine butter, oats, brown sugar and flour and sprinkle mixture over apples.

Bake for 40 to 45 minutes or until apples are tender and topping is nicely browned.

Optional: Add 1 teaspoon cinnamon and ½ cup raisins or dried cranberries to apples before sprinkling with topping.

Lickity-Split Apple Crisp

This apple dish could not be easier. It is a great standby dessert if you keep the pie filling and oatmeal on hand. It can be put together in minutes and there is little clean-up.

2 (20 ounce) cans apple pie filling
3 (1.62 ounce) packets cinnamon-spice instant oatmeal
½ cup flour
½ cup firmly packed brown sugar
½ cup (1 stick) butter or margarine, melted

Preheat oven to 350°.

Pour apple pie filling in 9 x 13-inch baking dish.

Combine oatmeal, flour and brown sugar in bowl. Stir in melted butter and mix well.

Crumble mixture over pie filling.

Bake for 45 minutes or until top is nicely browned.

For additional flavor, sprinkle a teaspoon of apple pie spice over apple pie filling before the topping. You may also add ½ cup round pecans to the topping mixture. And, last but not least, serve it warm with a scoop of vanilla ice cream for the ultimate taste treat.

Honey-Glazed Apple Turnovers

This quick, easy dessert uses ingredients that are frequently on hand. Keep a box of puff pastry in the freezer to serve these turnovers as a warm dessert or a special breakfast dish.

½ cup finely chopped walnuts
2 tablespoons dried currants or raisins
⅓ cup plus ¼ cup honey
1 large braeburn or Granny Smith apple
1 (17.3 ounce) package (2 count) puff pastry, thawed

Preheat oven at 375°.

In small bowl, combine walnuts, currants and ⅓ cup honey.

Peel, core and dice apple into small pieces. Add to honey mixture and mix well.

Remove pastry sheet from refrigerator and unroll sheet onto lightly floured surface. Cut into fourths (divide in half vertically and horizontally).

Divide half honey-apple mixture among 4 squares, placing mixture on one-half of each square leaving ½-inch border on sides.

Fold pastry in half diagonally. Try to keep mixture within a triangle shape on pastry half.

Moisten two sides of pastry half containing filling, gently lift corner of unfilled side and place it on corner of filled side.

Line up pastry edges by stretching in place, if needed and gently press together to seal.

Place each turnover on lightly greased baking sheet and bake for 15 minutes.

(continued on next page)

(continued)

Warm remaining honey and drizzle over each turnover before serving.
Serve warm.

*Optional: For more robust flavor, add 1 teaspoon cinnamon to apple mixture
before placing on puff pastry.*

*These turnovers look very nice when baked with an egg wash, which gives
them a nice shiny coating. Lightly brush a beaten egg over the surface of
each turnover before placing in the oven. Everyone will be impressed.*

You may also serve this with Rum Raisin Sauce on page 12.

Currants

There are two different fruits called currants. The currant used in this
recipe looks like a tiny, dark raisin and comes from the zante grape, which
originated in Greece. This type of currant is used mainly in baked goods.

The other type of currant is a tiny berry related to the gooseberry, which
comes in several colors. This type of currant is typically used in preserves,
syrups and liqueurs or for eating out of hand.

Apple Dumplings

1½ cups firmly packed brown sugar, divided
¼ cup chopped pecans
2 tablespoons butter or margarine, softened
6 baking apples, cored
1 (9 inch) double pastry shell
½ cup water

Preheat oven to 425°.

Mix ½ cup sugar, pecans and butter in bowl. Spoon into each apple.

Roll half pastry to ⅛-inch thickness. Cut into 3 squares approximately 7 inches.

Wrap 1 pastry square around each apple and pinch edges to seal.

Place remaining 1 cup of sugar and water in saucepan over medium heat and stir until sugar dissolves. Pour syrup over dumplings.

Bake for 35 to 40 minutes or until tender, basting occasionally with syrup.

For even more flavorful dumplings, add 2 teaspoons cinnamon or apple pie spice along with sugar, pecans and butter.

Quick and Easy Apple Pastries

1 (17.3 ounce) package (2 count) pastry sheets, divided
½ cup apricot or raspberry jam
3 small Granny Smith apples, peeled, cored, very thinly sliced
2 tablespoons sugar
½ teaspoon cinnamon

On lightly floured surface, roll out 1 sheet of pastry dough to ⅛-inch thickness. Cut into 15 (3-inch) squares.

Lay squares on baking sheets. Turn edges up slightly.

Spread each square with small spoonful of jam.

Place apple slices attractively on top of jam.

In small bowl, combine sugar and cinnamon and stir well to mix. Sprinkle each pastry with cinnamon-sugar mixture.

Bake at 350° for 15 to 20 minutes until pastries are nicely browned around edges.

Phyllo Dough

"Phyllo," pronounced "FEE-loh" means "leaf" in Greek. It refers to layers of paper-thin pastry dough used in Greek and Near Eastern cooking. You may find packaged frozen phyllo dough in the freezer section of your grocery store, usually located with the pie shells.

Phyllo dries out very quickly when uncovered, you must work fast when using it. There are a few simple things to do to make it much easier to work.

- If phyllo dough is frozen, thaw it at room temperature for a couple of hours before handling.

- Assemble all ingredients before opening package and open it only when you're ready to make triangles.

- Work in batches. Once you remove three sheets you'll work with for one batch, immediately cover the unused phyllo with plastic wrap and then a damp towel.

- Use a very soft bristle pastry brush to spread butter over the sheets and start by lightly brushing the edges first and then work toward the center of the dough.

- Re-roll and wrap any remaining dough not needed and place it back in freezer

Storage:

An unopened phyllo dough package can be stored in the refrigerator for up to 1 month. Once opened, use within 2 to 3 days. Frozen phyllo can be stored for up to 1 year. Thaw overnight in refrigerator. Refreezing phyllo will make it brittle.

Phyllo Chocolate Triangles

1½ cups coarsely chopped toasted pecans
4 ounces semi-sweet chocolate, grated
¼ teaspoon ground cinnamon
15 (9 x 14-inch) sheets phyllo dough
5-6 tablespoons butter, melted

Combine toasted pecans, chocolate and cinnamon in medium bowl and stir to blend.

Preheat oven to 400°.

Use 3 sheets phyllo dough at 1 time and keep remainder covered with damp towel in plastic. Place 1 sheet on clean, dry surface and brush lightly with melted butter.

Place a second sheet on top and brush it in the same way. Repeat with a third sheet of phyllo. Be sure and work fast to assemble the buttered pastry. The dough dries out very quickly when it's uncovered.

Using pastry wheel, cut layered dough into 5 strips, each approximately 2½-inches wide. They will be 9 inches long.

Take teaspoonful chocolate mixture and place about 1½ inches up from end of strip. Take end of strip and overlap filling to form a triangle.

Fold triangle up and over and continue to fold as you would a flag. Place triangle seam side down on an ungreased baking sheet.

When baking sheet is full, lightly brush surface of each triangle with butter and bake for about 12 minutes until triangles are nicely browned and crisp.

Remove from oven and let triangles cool. Store in covered container for up to 2 days.

Yield 25 triangles.

Peach Phyllo Rolls with Caramel Sauce

These deliciously flaky pastries look like egg rolls, but contain sweet peaches. The caramel sauce complements them perfectly.

3 large peaches, peeled
8 tablespoons butter, divided
¼ cup plus 3 tablespoons sugar
18 (9 x 14-inch) sheets phyllo dough

Dice peaches into pieces about ½-inch square. Place in medium saucepan with 2 tablespoons butter and 3 tablespoons sugar.

Cook over medium heat until peaches are softened, about 4 minutes. Remove from heat and set aside.

Preheat oven to 400°.

Melt remaining butter in separate saucepan.

Remove 3 sheets phyllo dough and keep remaining sheets wrapped in plastic and covered with damp towel to prevent them from drying out.

Work quickly, lay 1 piece of dough on clean dry surface and brush lightly with butter using soft pastry brush, working from edges inward.

Place second sheet of dough on top lining edges up and brush in same way. Repeat with third piece of phyllo dough.

Place one-sixth peach mixture about 2 inches from short end leaving about 1½-inch dough border.

Lift short end of dough over peach mixture and then lift each side, bringing it over peach mixture.

(continued on next page)

(continued)

Roll up (like an egg roll) and place seam side down on ungreased baking sheet.

Repeat with remaining mixture and pastry sheets to make 5 more rolls.

Bake for 10 minutes, until rolls are nicely browned.

Caramel Sauce:

Place remaining ¼ cup sugar and 3 tablespoons water in small, heavy saucepan. Cook over medium heat, stirring constantly, until sugar dissolves.

Turn heat to medium high and let mixture simmer rapidly until it becomes a deep amber color, about 10 minutes.

Do not stir, but swirl pan occasionally and brush down the sides of pan with wet pastry brush.

Remove from heat and quickly whisk in cream carefully. Mixture will bubble.

Place back on medium heat and stir frequently until mixture thickens and caramel melts.

Makes about ½ cup.

Pour caramel sauce over rolls while they are still warm. Serve immediately

Cenci

The word "cenci" in Italian means rags. These little pastries are shaped into knots, fried and dusted with powdered sugar.

3 cups flour
2 tablespoons powdered sugar plus extra for dusting
1½ teaspoons baking powder
4 eggs
Grated peel of 1 small orange

Sift flour, powdered sugar and baking powder together in large bowl.

Make well and put eggs and orange peel into it.

Beat eggs and incorporate flour mixture from around sides a little at a time until dough is workable.

Knead dough for about 2 minutes and then divide into fourths. Wrap each fourth and set it aside for about 20 minutes to rest.

Heat oil in deep, heavy frying pan or fryer to 375°.

Roll out each fourth of dough very thinly into a rectangle. (Keep remaining dough covered until ready to use.)

Use pastry cutter or sharp knife to cut dough into strips ½ inches wide by 7 inches long.

Carefully tie each strip into loose knot and fry until golden brown.

Drain on paper towels and dust with powdered sugar. Serve immediately or soon after making.

Heavenly Mocha Ganache Bites

Crispy, flaky phyllo pastry shells filled with soft, fudge-like mocha-flavored chocolate become bite-size chocolate treats, which are a snap to make and look very elegant. With only 3 ingredients, you will have a party dish that is sure to draw rave reviews.

¼ cup heavy whipping cream
1 (3.5 ounce) mocha-flavored chocolate bar
1 (2.1 ounce) box (15 shells) miniature,
pre-baked phyllo dough shells

Place cream in small, heavy saucepan over low heat. Break chocolate bar into pieces and add to cream.

Stir constantly until chocolate melts and mixture is smooth.

Remove from heat and immediately pour into phyllo dough shells. Use measuring cup with spout.

Chill until chocolate sets, about 1½ hours. Keep chilled until ready to serve.

Optional: For a final flourish, you may add a chocolate-covered coffee bean to the top of each pastry after filling.

Variations: You may also add a little variety by selecting different flavors of chocolate bars, such as hazelnut and mint. Do another batch using white chocolate instead of the milk chocolate and mix the 2 on a tray.

Chocolate-Filled Cream Puffs

1 cup water
½ cup (1 stick) butter
1 cup flour
4 eggs
1 (22 ounce) plus 1 (8 ounce) container
chocolate pudding (3½-4 cups)
1 cup milk chocolate chips, melted

Preheat oven to 400°.

Combine water and butter in medium saucepan and bring to a boil. When butter melts, remove pan from heat.

Stir in flour until mixture forms a ball and pulls away from sides of pan.

Beat in eggs until mixture is smooth. (At first it will appear sort of curdled, but after you begin to beat it, it will become very smooth.)

Drop by rounded tablespoonfuls onto ungreased baking sheet.

Bake for 35 minutes or until cream puffs are well browned.

Remove from oven and cool to room temperature.

Cut tops off cream puffs and set aside. Fill with chocolate pudding and replace tops.

Drizzle melted chocolate over each cream puff.

(continued on next page)

(continued)

Tip: Cream puff shells keep very well. Make them the day before and fill them the day you need them, so they will be very fresh (and not soggy). If you are not going to fill the shells immediately, keep them covered or in a sealed plastic bag once they have completely cooled.

Tip: As an alternative to using a pastry bag, it is easy to fill cream puffs by putting the pudding in a sturdy plastic bag and cutting about ¹/₈ inch off the corner. This makes a handy, neat way to pipe the pudding into the puffs. Do this with chocolate as well. Put chips in bag and melt them in the microwave on HALF power for about 2 minutes, kneading bag after each minute. Snip off a tiny corner of bag and squeeze melted chocolate out in a steady stream over the cream puffs.

Custard Filling

Additional fillings may be used with these cream puffs and here is one that is delicious.

3 egg yolks
½ cup sugar
2 tablespoons cornstarch
2 cups half-and-half

Combine egg yolks, sugar and cornstarch in top of double boiler over simmering water.

Stir to blend into smooth paste and gradually add half-and-half as you stir.

Cook, stirring frequently, for 10 to 13 minutes until mixture thickens to the consistency of pudding. Remove from heat and cool before filling cream puffs.

Tarte Tatin

This very famous French, upside-down apple tart is made by covering the bottom of a shallow baking dish with butter and sugar, apples and a pastry crust. While baking, the sugar and butter create a delicious caramel sauce that becomes the topping when the tart is inverted onto a serving plate.

The tart was created more than 100 years ago by two French sisters who lived in the Loire Valley and earned their living preparing the dessert. The French call this dessert "tarte des demoiselles Tatin", the "tart of two unmarried women named Tatin".

A good Tarte Tatin depends a lot on the choice of the apple, which should be sharp, firm and juicy. Braeburn, La Belle de Boskoop, Granny Smith and Fuji are all good varieties.

You also need a heavy-bottomed, non-stick skillet with an ovenproof handle. Any good, cast-iron skillet will work fine.

(continued on next page)

(continued)

Tarte Tatin

½ cup (1 stick) butter
½ cup sugar
1 (8-inch) skillet
3-4 baking apples
1 (7.3 ounce) package (2 count) puff pastry dough, divided

Melt butter and sugar in heavy 8-inch ovenproof skillet, stirring occasionally until sugar dissolves.

Cut bases from apples and quarter to give quarters flat bottom to rest on.

Place apple quarters on end in pan, fitting them snugly in attractive pattern. (It is easier to place one in middle and others around it, filling it gaps with any leftover pieces.)

Cook over medium high heat for 20 minutes (do not stir), until apples are fork-tender and sugar begins to caramelize (the syrup should turn deep amber and become syrupy).

Remove from heat and place sheet of puff pastry over apples. Gently tuck pastry in around sides of apples using butter knife.

Preheat oven to 400°.

Place skillet in oven and bake for 20 to 25 minutes (until pastry is nicely browned).

Remove from oven and let cool for 10 minutes, then invert onto serving plate.

Serve warm or at room temperature.

Raspberry-Nectarine Tart

This pretty, square tart looks great when made with white flesh nectarines, because their pink tinged edges complement the color of the raspberries. They are also slightly firmer and sweeter, however any nectarines will work.

**¼ cup plus 2 tablespoons sugar
2 teaspoons cornstarch
3 nectarines, peeled, pitted, sliced
½ pint raspberries, washed, dried
1 (17.3 ounce) package (2 count) puff pastry, thawed**

Preheat oven to 400°.

In small bowl, combine sugar and cornstarch and stir to blend.

Place nectarines and raspberries in large bowl.

Sprinkle cornstarch mixture over and gently toss fruit to coat. (Take care not to mash raspberries.)

Place 1 puff pastry sheet on lightly greased baking sheet.

Use slotted spoon to drain juices and spoon half fruit mixture evenly onto pastry sheet leaving 2-inch border. Arrange fruit attractively.

Lift 1 side puff pastry over fruit filling. Repeat on remaining 3 sides. You may need to pinch corners slightly to keep filling from seeping out.

Sprinkle remaining 2 tablespoons sugar over dough border.

Bake for 20 minutes. Remove from oven and cool before serving.

Repeat with other pastry sheet and remaining half of fruit filling.

(continued on next page)

(continued)

Nectarines or "nectar of the gods" are a variety of peach. Nectarines usually have smooth, dark orange or red skin and tend to be smaller than peaches. They are ready to eat when they smell sweet and "give" a little when touched. Nectarines may also be enjoyed when they are slightly firm, particularly the Zee Sweet varieties.

Tip for peeling nectarines: Make small "x" in bottom of fruit, place in boiling water for 1 minute and put in ice water. When it is cool enough to handle, you may slip skin off.

Tarts

A tart is a pastry crust with shallow sides, a filling and no top crust. The filling may be sweet like a fruit or sweet custard or savory like meat, cheese or savory custard. Depending on type of tart, its pastry shell can either be baked first and then filled or filled and then baked.

Tarts come in different sizes. They can be bite-size, individual-size or full-size. You will find a variety of tart recipes in this cookbook, in all different sizes.

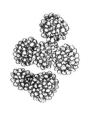

Fresh Peach Tarts

1 (8 ounce) package (8 count) frozen tart shells, thawed
⅔ cup ground pecans plus 8 pecan halves
7 tablespoons lightly packed brown sugar, divided
2 tablespoons butter, melted
2 large, firm, ripe peaches

Preheat oven to 375°.

Put tart shells on baking sheet and bake for 5 minutes. Remove from oven and set aside.

Turn oven up to 400°. Place pecans in small bowl and add 6 tablespoons sugar and butter. Stir well and set aside.

Slice peaches into ¼-inch wedges and cut wedges in half to make pieces small enough to fit easily into tart shells.

Combine with remaining 1 tablespoon sugar and stir until peaches are coated.

Divide peach mixture among tart shells.

Spoon pecan topping evenly over peaches. Place whole pecan half on top of each for garnish.

Bake 15 minutes or until topping and edges of tart are nicely browned.

Remove from oven and cool to lukewarm or room temperature before serving.

Fresh Lemon Tarts

1 (8 ounce) package (8 count) frozen tart shells
⅔ cup fresh lemon juice
½ cup sugar
3 tablespoons sour cream
4 eggs

Preheat oven to 375°.

Bake tart shells according to package directions. Set aside to cool.

Whisk lemon juice and sugar in medium bowl. Whisk in sour cream.

Whisk in eggs 2 at a time until well blended. Pour mixture into tart shells.

Bake tarts until filling is set, about 30 minutes.

Cool tarts completely on cooling rack and chill at least 1 hour. If desired, garnish each tart with dollop of whipped cream and lemon slices.

Lemony Cheese Tarts

2 large lemons
1 (8 ounce) package (8 count) frozen tart shells, thawed
3 eggs
¾ cup sugar, divided
1 (8 ounce) container mascarpone cheese, softened

Squeeze ½ cup juice from lemons and grate 1 tablespoon of zest from peel. Set aside.

Bake tart shells according to package directions. Set aside to cool.

Beat eggs lightly and place in top of double boiler. Whisk in ½ cup sugar, lemon zest and lemon juice.

Cook in double boiler over simmering water, whisking constantly, until mixture is smooth and slightly thickened, about 10 minutes. The mixture is ready when it coats the back of a spoon and leaves a trail when you drag your finger across it.

Remove top of double boiler from heat and set aside to cool.

In medium bowl, beat cheese until light and fluffy. Gradually beat in remaining ¼ cup sugar.

Fold cooled lemon mixture into cheese mixture in several additions. Chill and divide among prepared tart shells.

Lime-Cheesecake Tarts

2 small limes
6 miniature graham cracker crust pie shells
1 (8 ounce) package cream cheese, softened
⅓ cup sugar
1 egg

Squeeze 3 tablespoons lime juice, grate 1 teaspoon zest from peel and set aside.

Preheat oven to 400°.

Bake empty shells for 5 minutes. Remove from oven and set aside. Reduce oven temperature to 325°.

In mixing bowl, beat cream cheese until smooth.

Add sugar and beat until light and fluffy. Beat in egg, then lime juice and grated lime zest.

Spoon cheese mixture into pie shells and bake for 30 to 35 minutes or until knife inserted in center comes out clean.

Remove from oven and cool. Chill until ready to serve.

If desired, serve with dollop of whipped cream on top and sprinkle of grated lime zest.

Caramel-Pecan Tarts in Chocolate Shells

¾ cup sugar
⅓ cup water
⅓ cup whipping cream
5 tablespoons butter
1 cup coarsely chopped pecans
8 chocolate shells

Place sugar and water in medium heavy saucepan over low heat. Stir until sugar dissolves.

Increase heat to medium high and boil until syrup becomes amber colored, about 10 minutes. Occasionally brush down sides of pan with wet pastry brush and swirl pan from time to time, but do not stir.

Remove from heat and stir in cream and butter. Mixture will bubble furiously.

Return pan to low heat and stir until caramel is smooth and color gets deeper, about 5 minutes.

Remove from heat and stir in pecans.

Let mixture cool slightly and chill, uncovered, for about 20 minutes until it is cold, but not firm.

Pour into chocolate shells and serve.

Chocolate Shells

These stunning little chocolate cups are easy to make and hold a variety of fillings. They look very sophisticated and elegant. The recipe describes how to make chocolate "muffin cups", but you may use the same technique to create smaller versions with petite four cups or tartlet pans.

**16 ounces semi-sweet baking chocolate
4 foil muffin cup liners
Small, soft pastry brush**

Melt chocolate and stir until smooth. Use top of double boiler over simmering water, microwave or stovetop.

Put foil liners into muffin cups.

Pour 1 to 2 teaspoons chocolate in muffin cup. Gently turn so chocolate coats inside. If necessary, use pastry brush to paint chocolate on sides of cup. Leave border at top of liner for handle when chocolate is set.

(It is important to get an even coating of chocolate. If you get really good coverage from the first coating, it won't be necessary to do a second. The chocolate coating needs to be thick enough, especially on the sides to handle. If you see thin spots on sides, let chocolate set, melt another 2 ounces chocolate and brush second layer over first.)

Chill cup and coat remaining ones with chocolate. Chill cups until chocolate is set. Carefully and quickly peel foil liner away from chocolate. Keeps cups chilled until ready to use.

(continued on next page)

(continued)

Chocolate Tartlet Shells

To create decorative tartlet shells, use 6 (3½-inch) shells that are very shallow. (Shells with non-stick coating work well.) Just 4 ounces chocolate is enough for this size and quantity. Coat insides with chocolate and freeze for several minutes. Use fork to gently pull down on inside around edges until chocolate releases.

Chill until ready to serve.

Strawberry-Zabaglione Tarts

Zabaglione (also spelled Zabaione) is a rich Italian custard made from egg yolks, sugar and Marsala wine. The light, frothy custard is perfect served as a sauce over cake, fruit, ice cream or pastry.

6 egg yolks
½ cup sugar
4 tablespoons sweet Marsala wine
1½ cups sliced strawberries
1 (10 ounce) package (8 count) frozen tart shells, baked, cooled

Whisk egg yolks and sugar in medium bowl until well blended. Whisk in Marsala.

Place mixture in top of double boiler over simmering water and whisk vigorously and constantly until mixture increases in volume and thickens.

Scrape sides of pan frequently as you whisk. (Make sure water only simmers to avoid eggs curdling.) Mixture is cooked when it coats whisk.

Remove from heat and cool slightly.

Place strawberries in tart shells. Spoon custard over strawberries. Chill until ready to serve. This dish may be made several hours in advance.

Tip: Frozen tarts will be with the frozen pie shells in grocery store.

Black Walnut-Maple Tartlets

These flavorful little treats pair the distinctive flavors of black walnut and maple in delicate, flaky little pastry shells small enough to eat in two bites. They are easy to make, especially since the pastry shells are already made and baked.

1 (14 ounce) can sweetened condensed milk
½ cup real maple syrup
½ cup chopped black walnuts, toasted
2½ (2.1 ounce) packages miniature phyllo dough shells

Combine sweetened condensed milk and maple syrup in heavy medium saucepan over medium heat. Stir until well blended.

When mixture starts to bubble, reduce heat slightly, cook and stir constantly until mixture thickens, about 10 minutes.

Stir in walnuts and remove from heat.

Immediately fill prepared shells. Cool before serving.

Makes about 45.

Tip: To toast walnuts, place in a single layer on baking sheet and bake at 350° for about 5 minutes until nuts are lightly browned. Remove from oven and cool.

Strawberry-Lemon Curd Tartlets

These tartletts are 5-minute wonders!

1 (8 ounce) package (8 count) frozen tart shells, baked, cooled
2 cups lemon curd
1 pint fresh strawberries, sliced
¼ cup seedless strawberry jam

Divide lemon curd among baked tart shells.

Place strawberry slices attractively on top.

Warm strawberry jam in microwave on MEDIUM HIGH for about 45 seconds and brush jam over strawberries with pastry brush for glaze.

Serve immediately.

Pavlovas

A Pavlova is a delicious dessert from Australia and New Zealand named after the great Russian ballerina Anna Pavlova. The actual country from which it originates is the subject of hot debate, but it is an absolutely fabulous dish regardless of who actually invented it. It consists of a meringue base that is crispy on the outside and soft in the middle, topped with whipped cream and fresh fruit (typically strawberries and kiwi).

Strawberry Pavlova

5 egg whites
1¾ cups sugar, divided
1 teaspoon vinegar
1½ cups whipping cream
2 pints strawberries, washed, hulled, halved

Preheat oven to 250°.

Prepare baking sheet by lining with foil or parchment paper. Use bowl or round baking dish as template, outline circle about 10 inches wide on foil or paper. Set aside.

To make meringue base beat egg whites on high speed until soft peaks form.

Gradually add 1½ cups sugar and continue to beat until mixture is white and glossy and stiff peaks form (about 10 minutes).

Add vinegar and beat on high speed for another 5 minutes.

Spread meringue mixture in circle on baking sheet. Keep sides straight and top as flat as possible. (A small, flexible spatula works well for this.)

(continued on next page)

(continued)

Draw spatula up sides of meringue circle to form "ribs", which will not only give finished look, but will also add some strength once it is baked.

Bake for 1 hour, then turn oven off and leave in oven for another couple of hours. (It will keep very well until you are not ready to assemble dessert. Simply keep it tightly covered until ready to use.)

When ready to assemble, carefully remove meringue base from foil or parchment paper and place on serving plate.

Beat whipping cream with remaining ½ cup sugar until soft peaks form. Spread evenly over surface of meringue base.

Arrange strawberries attractively on top and serve.

Tips:
The spatula should be a straight-sided spatula like type used for icing.

Almost any variety of fresh fruit in season will be wonderful. Although this dish is traditionally made with strawberries and kiwi, raspberries, blackberries, cherries or blueberries taste great.

For a festive presentation, arrange fruit in concentric circles. Put one whole strawberry in middle and arrange cut strawberries in circles around it, starting from middle and working outward. Place strawberries cut side down with their pointed ends facing outward.

When using more than one kind of fruit, alternate slices. For example, make ring of strawberries surrounded by ring of kiwi, then another strawberry ring, etc.

This dessert will keep for a day after making it. Although it is best to serve within a few hours of assembly, you may cover remainder and keep it refrigerated for up to two days.

Chocolate-Raspberry Pavlova

You can alter the flavor of the basic Pavlova with liqueur and fruit other than
strawberries to create a dessert that is just as delicious with a personality all its own.
In this version, chocolate and cherries are the featured ingredients, set off with a
chocolate liqueur whipped cream.

5 egg whites
1¾ cups sugar, divided
1 teaspoon vinegar
1½ cups whipping cream
¼ cup creme de cacao liqueur
1 (15.25 ounce) can cherries, well drained
1 (3.5 ounce) chocolate bar, grated

Follow instructions for Strawberry Pavlova on page 144, but add creme
de cacao along with whipping cream and remaining ½ cup sugar.

Beat until soft peaks form and spread evenly over surface of meringue
base.

Arrange cherries attractively on top and garnish with grated chocolate.

Cheese Blintzes

Blintzes are basically crepes containing sweet or savory fillings. As a dessert, they may be filled with sweetened cottage cheese or fruit, such as apple, cherry or blueberry. Once rolled, they are usually fried in oil and served with sour cream.

Cheese blintzes are the traditional meal for the Jewish festival of Shavu'ot, when dairy meals are traditionally eaten. They are also commonly eaten during Chanukah because they are cooked in oil. The word "blintz" comes from a Ukrainian word meaning "pancake".

2 cups dry cottage cheese
2 eggs, lightly beaten
¼ cup sugar
2 tablespoons lemon juice
10-12 dessert crepes (page 150)

Combine cottage cheese, eggs, sugar and lemon juice in medium bowl and stir until well blended.

Lay crepe out onto plate and spread some filling along 1 edge.

Fold each side in and tightly roll up, starting with edge containing filling. Repeat with remaining filling.

Chill at least 1 hour.

Just before serving, melt 2 tablespoons butter or oil in large heavy skillet.

Place blintzes in skillet, seam side down, and brown on both sides, turning once. (Add butter or oil as necessary.)

Serve with dollop of sour cream on the side and some fruit filling spooned on top.

Dessert Crepes

2 eggs
1 cup flour
2 tablespoons sugar
1 cup milk
1 tablespoon butter, melted

In medium bowl, beat eggs and then whisk in flour and sugar. Mix well and add a little milk to make a smooth paste.

Gradually add remaining milk, whisking after each addition, until mixture is smooth and has no lumps.

Whisk in butter.

Cover batter and refrigerate for 1 hour to chill.

When ready to cook, preheat small crepe pan or frying pan (with a 5" or 6" bottom and sloping sides) and brush with butter.

Pour from 1 to 2 tablespoons batter into pan (depending upon size of pan) and tilt pan to cover entire bottom. Cook crepe for a couple of minutes, until it begins to brown.

Turn it over and cook for another minute or less on other side. Turn out of pan onto platter.

Repeat with remaining batter, stacking crepes as they come out of pan.

Cover with plastic wrap and chill until needed.

Makes about 12 crepes.

Chocolate Crepes

2 eggs
½ cup flour
2 tablespoons cocoa
3 tablespoons sugar
1 cup half-and-half

In medium bowl, beat the eggs and add flour and cocoa. Stir well to blend.

Stir in sugar. Gradually whisk in half-and-half until mixture is smooth.

Cover and chill for at least 1 hour.

When ready to cook, preheat small crepe pan or frying pan with 5 to 6-inch bottom and sloping sides and brush with butter.

Pour 1 to 2 tablespoons batter into pan (depending upon size of pan) and tilt pan to cover entire bottom. Let crepe cook for about 2 minutes until it begins to brown.

Turn crepe over and cook for another minute or less on other side. Turn out of pan onto platter.

Repeat with remaining batter, stacking crepes as they come out of pan.

Cover with plastic wrap and chill until needed.

Makes 12 crepes.

Fresh Strawberry Crepes

1 pound fresh strawberries
2 tablespoons powdered sugar
10 to 12 dessert crepes (page 148)
4 ounces (½ cup) sour cream, divided
½ cup (or more) strawberry preserves, warmed

Wash and hull strawberries. Slice and place in bowl or container.

Sprinkle powdered sugar over and gently stir. Chill at least 1 hour.

To assemble, spread 1 teaspoon sour cream in middle of dessert crepe.

Place 1 to 2 tablespoons fresh strawberries over sour cream and roll up.

Spoon strawberry preserves over top. Serve immediately.

Makes 10 to 12 crepes.

Option: Another great way to serve strawberry crepes is with brown sugar in place of strawberry preserves. Instead of putting sour cream on inside, roll up crepe with only strawberries and put dollop of sour cream on outside. Sprinkle about 1 tablespoon brown sugar over entire crepe.

Black Forest Crepes

1 cup whipping cream
10-12 chocolate crepes (page149)
⅛ cup cherry liqueur
1 (21 ounce) can cherry pie filling
3.5-4 ounces premium dark chocolate, grated

Beat whipping cream until stiff peaks form and set aside.

Prepare Dessert Crepes on page 148.

To assemble crepes, place crepe on plate and sprinkle 1 teaspoon cherry liqueur over.

Drop 1 to 2 heaping tablespoons cherry pie filling down center and roll up.

Pipe whipped cream over rolled crepe or spoon 1 to 2 tablespoons over crepe.

Sprinkle grated chocolate on top for garnish. Repeat with remaining crepes.

Makes 10 to 12 crepes.

Crepes Suzette

This delectable dessert has a warm, buttery-orange flavored sauce. The crepes taste great by themselves, but are much better with a scoop of premium vanilla ice cream on the side.

8 dessert crepes
2 oranges, divided
⅓ cup butter
⅓ cup sugar
4 ounces Grand Marnier or other orange liqueur

Grate peel of 1 orange for zest and squeeze juice from 2 oranges.

Cream butter, sugar and orange zest.

Place in large chafing dish over medium high heat and cook until mixture bubbles. Continue to cook, stirring occasionally, until mixture begins to brown.

Add freshly squeezed orange juice, a little at a time, stirring after each addition. Stir in 2 ounces orange liqueur. Cook until slightly thickened.

Working with 1 crepe at a time fold each crepe in half and place it in dish, turning it over to coat both sides. Use 2 forks to fold crepe in half again and move to side of dish. Repeat procedure for all crepes.

Heat remaining orange liqueur in microwave on HIGH for 45 seconds and pour into dish. Do not stir, carefully ignite liqueur. Spoon flaming sauce over crepes and serve.

Plan to serve two per person.

Famous Flaming Desserts

Flambé [flahm-BAY] is French for "flamed" or "flaming". This dramatic presentation consists of sprinkling certain foods with warmed liquor and igniting at the dining table so guests may see the preparation. Warm liquor is poured over certain foods and ignited to create the flambe.

Bananas Foster

This elegant dish was created at New Orleans's Brennan's Restaurant in the 1950's in honor of Richard Foster, a regular customer. Sliced bananas are quickly sauteed in a mixture of rum, brown sugar and banana liqueur and served with vanilla ice cream. This simplified version omits the banana liqueur, but doesn't suffer for it.

3 large bananas
½ cup (1 stick) butter
½ cup firmly packed brown sugar
⅛ teaspoon cinnamon
⅓ cup rum

Peel bananas and slice in half at a diagonal. Slice each half vertically to equal 12 pieces and set aside.

Combine butter, brown sugar and cinnamon in medium saucepan over medium high heat.

Stir until thickened, about 3 to 4 minutes. Add bananas and saute until tender about 2 minutes, coating them with sauce as they cook.

Heat rum in microwave on HIGH for 30 seconds.

Pour over mixture and carefully ignite.

Spoon mixture over bananas until flames die and immediately serve over vanilla ice cream or pound cake.

Cherries Jubilee

If you want a dramatic, but simple end to a lovely meal and to impress your friends, serve Cherries Jubilee. It is a simple 5-minute recipe that makes a lifetime memory with an impressive flambe right at your table.

Orange juice
1 (15.25 ounce) can pitted, dark sweet cherries, drained, syrup reserved
2 tablespoons cornstarch
2 tablespoons sugar
⅓ cup orange liqueur

Add enough orange juice to reserved cherry syrup to equal 1½ cups liquid.

Add about two tablespoons liquid to cornstarch and stir to make a smooth paste.

Combine reserved syrup mixture, sugar and cornstarch paste in chafing dish.

Cook and stir over medium heat until thick, about 4 minutes.

Add cherries to mixture in pan and stir.

Heat orange liqueur in the microwave on HIGH for about 1½ minutes.

Pour over cherries without stirring. Ignite and stir until flames subside.

Spoon over vanilla ice cream or brownies.

Tip: Use Kirsch or brandy instead of orange liqueur for the traditional flavoring.

Cherries Jubilee In A Flash

This is about as simple as it gets. It's wonderful over vanilla ice cream.

1 (20 ounce) can cherry pie filling
¼-½ cup brandy
Vanilla ice cream

Pour cherry pie filling in chafing dish or skillet.

Cook and stir over medium heat until hot.

In small saucepan, heat brandy until slightly warm; do not overheat.

Pour over pie filling. Carefully ignite brandy.

Gently shake pan back and forth to increase flame.

Spoon immediately over ice cream.

Tip: For a non-alcoholic sauce, omit brandy. Flame by soaking 6 sugar cubes in orange extract for 5 minutes. Place soaked cubes on top of hot pie filling. Ignite cubes just before serving.

Island-Volcano Flambe

3 large oranges
1 (20 ounce) can crushed pineapple with juice
3 teaspoons cornstarch
¼ cup rum
1 quart vanilla ice cream

Squeeze ½ cup juice from oranges and grate peel to equal 1 teaspoon.

In skillet or chafing dish stir together orange juice, orange peel and crushed pineapple with juice over medium-low heat.

Add cornstarch and cook until mixture bubbles and becomes slightly thick to sauce consistency.

Heat rum slightly in separate saucepan. Ignite and pour over pineapple mixture in chafing dish.

When flame subsides, spoon over ice cream.

Cookies & Candies

Potato Chip Crunchies

1 cup (2 sticks) margarine, softened
⅔ cups sugar
1 teaspoon vanilla
1½ cups flour
½ cup crushed potato chips

Cream margarine, sugar and vanilla and stir in flour.

Carefully fold in potato chips.

Drop by teaspoonfuls on ungreased baking sheet.

Bake at 350° for about 12 minutes or until lightly brown.

Easy Sand Tarts

1 cup (2 sticks) butter, softened
¾ cup powdered sugar
2 cups sifted flour
1 cup chopped pecans
1 teaspoon vanilla

In mixing bowl cream butter and sugar. Slowly add flour, pecans and vanilla.

Roll into crescents and place on ungreased baking sheet.

Bake at 325° for 20 minutes. Roll in extra powdered sugar after tarts have cooled.

Mexican Wedding Cookies

1 cup (2 sticks) butter or margarine
1 cup powdered sugar, divided
½ teaspoon vanilla
1¾ cups flour
½ cup chopped pecans or walnuts

Preheat oven to 350°.

Cream butter and ¾ cup sugar. Beat in vanilla, flour and nuts.

Cover and chill for about 1 hour.

Shape spoonful dough into 1-inch balls.

Place 2 inches apart on ungreased baking sheet and bake for 20 minutes.

Remove from oven and transfer to cooling rack. When cool, roll in remaining ½ cup powdered sugar.

Butterscotch Haystacks

1 (6 ounce) package chocolate chips
1 (6 ounce) package butterscotch chips
1 cup salted peanuts
1 can chow mein noodles

In large saucepan, melt chocolate and butterscotch chips.

Add peanuts and noodles and mix well

Drop by teaspoonfuls on wax paper.

Chill to harden.

Butterscotch Sweets

½ cup butterscotch chips
¼ cup flaked coconut
2 tablespoon chopped nuts
1 (8 ounce) can crescent dinner rolls
Powdered sugar

Preheat oven to 375°.

In small bowl mix butterscotch chips, coconut and nuts.

Unroll dough to form 8 triangles.

Sprinkle 1 heaping tablespoon butterscotch mixture on top of each triangle.

Roll each triangle into jellyroll.

Place rolls, seam side down, on ungreased cookie sheet.

Bake 10 to 12 minutes or until golden brown.

Sprinkle with powdered sugar.

Disappearing Cookies

1 (18 ounce) box butter cake mix
1 (3.4 ounce) package butterscotch instant pudding mix
1 cup oil
1 egg, beaten
1¼ cups chopped pecans

By hand, stir together cake mix and pudding mix and slowly add oil.

Add egg and mix thoroughly. Stir in pecans.

With teaspoon scoop cookie dough on baking sheet about 2 inches apart.

Bake at 350° for 8 or 9 minutes. Do not overcook.

Easy Sugar Cookies

1 (8 ounce) package cream cheese, softened
¾ cup sugar
1 cup (2 sticks) butter or margarine
½ teaspoon lemon extract
2½ cups flour

In medium bowl, combine cream cheese with sugar, butter and lemon extract. Beat until well blended.

Add flour and mix thoroughly. Cover and chill several hours or overnight.

When ready to bake, preheat oven to 375° and roll dough out on lightly floured surface to ⅛-inch thickness.

Cut shapes with cookie cutter and place on ungreased baking sheet.

Bake 6 to 8 minutes. Remove from oven and let cookies cool for 1 minute on baking sheet then transfer to cooling rack.

Optional: Before baking, lightly brush cookies with beaten egg and sprinkle with colored sugar or candy.

Snappy Almond-Sugar Cookies

1 cup (2 sticks) butter
1 cup plus 2 tablespoons sugar, divided
½ teaspoon almond extract
2 cups flour
1 cup chopped almonds

Cream butter, 1 cup sugar and almond extract until light and fluffy.

Slowly beat in flour and stir in nuts.

Shape dough into roll, wrap and chill well about 2 hours.

Preheat oven to 325°.

Slice roll into ¼-inch pieces and bake for 20 minutes.

Sprinkle with additional 2 tablespoons sugar while still hot.

Brown Sugar Cookies

1 cup (2 sticks) margarine, softened
¾ cup packed dark brown sugar
1 egg yolk
1 tablespoon vanilla
1¼ cups flour

In mixing bowl, beat margarine and gradually add brown sugar.

Add egg yolk and vanilla and beat well.

Add flour slowly and dash of salt and mix well.

Shape dough in 1-inch balls and chill 2 hours.

Place cookie dough on baking sheet and flatten each cookie with back of spoon.

Bake at 350° for 10 to 12 minutes.

Butter Pecan Dreams

1 cup (2 sticks) butter
4 tablespoons sugar
2 teaspoons vanilla
2 cups flour
2 cups chopped pecans

Preheat oven to 300°.

Cream butter and sugar. Add vanilla and mix.

Stir in flour and chopped pecans.

Roll dough into small balls and place on ungreased baking sheet.

Bake 30 to 45 minutes.

Remove from oven and roll in granulated sugar or powdered sugar.

Butter Pecan Cookies

1 cup (2 sticks) butter
½ cup firmly packed light brown sugar
1 large egg
2 cups flour
¾ cup chopped pecans, toasted

In medium bowl, beat butter and sugar until light and fluffy. Beat in egg.

Add flour and beat until well blended. Stir in pecans.

Divide dough in half. Shape each half into log 8 inches long and 1½-inches wide.

Cover each log well in either wax paper or plastic wrap and freeze until firm, about 30 minutes, or chill for up to 2 days.

When ready to bake, preheat oven to 350°.

Slice dough into pieces ⅓-inch thick and place slices 2 inches apart on ungreased baking sheet.

Bake for 15 minutes or until cookies are lightly browned around edges.

Remove from oven and transfer cookies to cooling rack.

Orange-Pecan Cookies

The cake mix makes these cookies a breeze because you have a head start.

2 cups pecan haves, divided
1 (18.25 ounce) orange cake mix
1 (8 ounce) carton vanilla yogurt
1 egg
2 tablespoons butter or margarine

Preheat oven to 350°.

Chop 1 cup pecans and set aside.

In large bowl, combine cake mix with yogurt, egg, butter and chopped pecans.

Beat on low speed just until blended.

Drop by rounded teaspoonfuls onto greased baking sheet.

Press whole pecan half on top of each cookie and bake 11 to 13 minutes or until lightly browned.

Remove from oven and let cookies cool for 1 minute, then transfer to cooling rack.

Old-Fashioned Peach Cookies

1 (20 ounce) can peach pie filling
1 (18 ounce) box yellow cake mix
2 eggs
1 cup finely chopped pecans
Sugar

In blender, blend pie filling until smooth.

In large bowl, combine pie filling, dry cake mix and eggs and blend well.

Stir in pecans.

Drop from tablespoon onto greased baking sheets.

Sprinkle with sugar.

Bake at 350° for 15 minutes or until lightly browned around edges.

Super-Fast Peanut Butter Drops

1 cup sugar
1 cup creamy or chunky peanut butter
1 egg
1 teaspoon vanilla

Preheat oven to 350°.

Combine all ingredients in medium bowl and mix well.

Drop by teaspoonfuls onto ungreased baking sheet.

Bake 13 to 15 minutes. Remove from oven and let cookies cool for 1 minute, then transfer to cooling rack.

Optional: Shape dough into 1 1/2-inch balls and roll in sugar. Place on baking sheet and flatten with fork, making a crisscross design, before baking.

Optional: Stir 1/2 cup miniature chocolate chips into dough before shaping cookies.

Peanut Butter Cookies

This cookie is fast, inexpensive and good and uses ingredients you usually have on hand.

1 cup crunchy or smooth peanut butter
1 cup sugar
1 egg
1 teaspoon vanilla

Preheat oven to 350°.

In medium bowl, combine peanut butter with sugar and mix well. Beat in egg and vanilla.

Roll heaping teaspoonfuls of dough into balls about 1½ inches in diameter. Flatten with fork dipped in sugar.

Place 2 inches apart on ungreased baking sheet and bake for 15 minutes.

Remove from oven and cool cookies on baking sheet for 1 minute before transferring to cooling rack.

Yields 2 dozen cookies.

Peanut Butter Surprise Cookies

1 egg, beaten
⅔ cup granulated sugar
⅓ cup packed brown sugar
1 cup chunky peanut butter
½ cup chopped dates

Blend egg, sugars and peanut butter and mix thoroughly.

Stir in dates and roll into 1-inch balls.

Place on ungreased baking sheet. Using back of fork, make criss-cross pattern on top of ball to flatten cookie.

Bake at 350° for about 12 minutes.

Peanut Butter Chip Cookies

1 (18 ounce) package prepared sugar cookie dough
½ cup creamy peanut butter
½ cup mini-chocolate chips
½ cup peanut butter chips
½ cup chopped peanuts

Beat together cookie dough and peanut butter in large bowl until blended and smooth.

Stir in chocolate chips, peanut butter chips and peanuts.

Drop dough by heaping tablespoons onto ungreased baking sheet.

Bake at 350° for 15 minutes.

Chocolate-Cherry Cookies

1 (18 ounce) cherry cake mix
¾ cup (1½ sticks) margarine, softened
2 eggs
1 cup miniature semi-sweet chocolate chips

Preheat oven to 350°.

In large bowl combine cake mix, butter and eggs and mix well.

Stir in chocolate chips.

Drop by rounded teaspoonfuls onto greased baking sheet.

Bake 10 to 12 minutes.

Cool slightly on baking sheet and remove to wire rack. Drizzle with glaze.

Glaze:

1 cup miniature semi-sweet chocolate chips
3 tablespoons shortening

Place in microwave-safe bowl and microwave on HIGH for 45 seconds and stir. (If chocolate melts and mixture is smooth, pour over cookies. If not, microwave another 15 to 20 seconds.)

Chocolate Cookie Sunday

½ cup (1 stick) margarine
1 (19 ounce) package chocolate sandwich cookies,
crushed, divided
½ gallon vanilla ice cream, softened, divided
2 jars fudge sauce, divided
1 (12 ounce) carton whipped topping

Melt margarine in 9 x 13-inch baking dish.

Reserve ½ cup crushed cookies for garnish and set aside.

Mix remaining cookies with margarine and press down to form crust in pan.

Spread half of ice cream over crust and pour jar fudge sauce over ice cream.

Repeat layers of ice cream and fudge sauce.

Top with whipped topping and sprinkle with remaining crumbs.

Garnish with Maraschino cherries if desired.

Makes 12 servings.

Kiss Me Chocolate

2 egg whites
⅔ cup sugar
1 teaspoon vanilla
1¼ cups chopped pecans
1 (6 ounce) package chocolate chips

Preheat oven at 375°.

Beat egg whites until very stiff. Blend in sugar, vanilla and dash salt.

Fold in pecans and chocolate chips.

Drop on shiny side of foil on baking sheet.

Put cookies in oven, TURN OVEN OFF AND LEAVE OVERNIGHT. If a little sticky, leave out in air to dry.

Coconut Bites

1 (12 ounce) package white chocolate baking chips
¼ cup (½ stick) margarine
16 large marshmallows
2 cups quick-cooking oats
1 cup flaked coconut

In saucepan over low heat, melt chocolate chips, margarine and marshmallows and stir until smooth.

Stir in oats and coconut and mix well.

Drop by rounded teaspoonfuls onto wax paper-lined baking sheets.

Chill until set.

Coconut-Chocolate Drops

1 cup sweetened condensed milk
4 cups coconut
⅔ cup miniature semi-sweet chocolate bits
1 teaspoon vanilla
½ teaspoon almond extract

Stir milk and coconut together to a gooey mixture.

Add chocolate bits, vanilla and almond and stir until well blended.

Drop by teaspoonfuls onto sprayed baking sheet.

Bake at 325° for 12 minutes.

Oatmeal-Chocolate Chip Cookies

1 (18 ounce) yellow cake mix
1 cup quick-cook rolled oats
¾ (1½ sticks) cup margarine, softened
2 eggs
1 cup semi-sweet chocolate chips

Preheat oven to 350°

In large bowl, combine cake mix, oats, margarine and eggs and beat until well blended.

Stir in chocolate chips.

Drop by teaspoonsful onto ungreased baking sheet.

Bake 10 to 12 minutes or until slightly brown.

Allow cookies to cool slightly, remove from baking sheet and cool completely on wire rack.

Charlie McRoons

We used to call these Chocolate Macaroons, but a sweet little 3-year-old renamed them for us.

1 (4 ounce) package sweet baking chocolate
2 egg whites
½ cup sugar
¼ teaspoon vanilla
1 (7 ounce) can flaked coconut

Divide egg whites and allow to reach room temperature.

Place chocolate in top of double boiler. Stir occasionally until chocolate melts and remove from heat to cool.

Beat egg whites at high speed for 1 minute. Gradually add sugar, 1 tablespoon at a time, beating until stiff peaks form, about 3 minutes.

Add chocolate and vanilla, beat well and stir in coconut.

Drop by teaspoonfuls onto baking sheet lined with brown paper.

Bake at 350° for 12 to 15 minutes. Allow to cool on brown paper placed on cooling rack.

Fast Chocolate Macarooons

These are really fast, delicious cookies.

4 (1 ounce) squares unsweetened chocolate, melted
1 (14 ounce) can sweetened condensed milk
2 teaspoons vanilla
1 (14 ounce) package flaked coconut

Preheat oven to 350°.

In large bowl, combine chocolate, sweetened condensed milk and vanilla.

Stir until well blended and evenly colored. Stir in coconut.

Drop by heaping teaspoonfuls about 2 inches apart onto greased baking sheet. Bake for 10 minutes.

Remove from oven and immediately transfer to cooling rack.

Makes 3½ dozen.

Ladyfingers

3 eggs, separated
1 teaspoon almond extract
⅓ cup sugar
½ cup cake flour
1 teaspoon baking powder

Beat egg yolks until thick and lemon-colored. Beat in almond extract.

In separate bowl, beat egg whites until stiff peaks form.

Continue beating and gradually add sugar until mixture is glossy and stiff.

Fold egg yolks into egg white mixture.

Sift flour and baking powder together and gently fold into egg white mixture.

Fill pastry bag and pipe mixture onto ungreased baking sheet in 3-inch lengths about 1 inch wide.

Bake 10 minutes. Remove from baking sheet and cool.

Almond-Meringue Cookies

2 egg whites
½ cup sugar
⅛ teaspoon almond extract

Preheat oven to 250°.

Line baking sheet with parchment paper or aluminum foil and set aside.

In medium bowl, beat egg whites on high speed until soft peaks form.

Gradually add sugar, beating after each addition, until mixture is glossy and holds stiff peaks.

Mix in almond extract on low speed. Drop by rounded teaspoonfuls about 1 inch apart onto baking sheet.

Bake for 1 hour. Turn oven off and leave cookies in oven for another 2 hours.

Remove from paper or foil and store tightly covered.

Meringues

Tips for making meringue:

Use a bowl that is completely grease-free. Any amount of fat will ruin a meringue. Any type of bowl is acceptable except plastic.

Separate eggs when they are cold, but allow egg white to sit at room temperature for 10 to 15 minutes for maximum volume.

Any yolk in the whites will deflate the meringue.

When beating meringue, beat to medium soft peaks and then begin adding sugar and continue to beat until whites are glossy and form stiff peaks.

Mocha-Chocolate Chip Meringues

3 egg whites
¾ cups sugar
4 tablespoons cocoa powder
1 tablespoons instant coffee
½ cup miniature chocolate chips

Preheat oven to 250°.

Line baking sheet with parchment paper or aluminum foil.

In large bowl, beat egg whites until soft peaks form.

Gradually add sugar about 2 tablespoons at a time and continue beating until stiff peaks form and mixture is glossy.

Combine cocoa powder and coffee in separate bowl.

Add to egg white mixture in several additions, beating on low speed after each addition.

Fold in chocolate chips.

Drop by rounded teaspoonfuls onto prepared baking sheet.

Bake for 1 hour. Turn oven off and leave cookies in another 2 hours.

Peanutty Chocolate Tortillas

4 (8 inch) flour tortillas
¼ cup peanut butter, divided
¼ cup marshmallow creme, divided
2 bananas, sliced, divided
½ cup milk chocolate chips, divided

Lighlty coat one side of each tortilla with cooking spray.

Place tortillas on work surface, coated side down.

Spread 1 tablespoon peanut butter over half tortilla. Spread 1 tablespoon marshmallow cream over other half of tortilla.

Place ¼ banana slices and 2 tablespoons chocolate chips over marshmallow creme and fold tortilla over to cover filling.

Heat large, non-stick skillet over medium heat.

Place each tortilla in skillet for 1 to 2 minutes or until golden brown and crispy.

Cool slightly and serve.

Amaretti

These are light, little Italian cookies with a crispy, melt-in-your-mouth outside
and a soft, chewy inside.

2 egg whites
Pinch salt
1 cup sugar
1 teaspoon almond extract
1 cup finely ground almonds

Preheat oven to 300°.

In medium bowl, beat egg whites with mixer until frothy and add salt.

Add sugar gradually, about 1 tablespoon at a time, while beating on high speed until stiff peaks form.

Fold in almond extract and almonds.

Drop by rounded teaspoonful onto prepared baking sheets and bake for 25 to 30 minutes until cookies are very lightly browned.

Remove from oven and let cookies cool.

Peel from paper and store in airtight container.

Yields about 2 to 2½ dozen cookies.

Cinnamon-Sugar Palmiers

²⁄₃ **cup turbinado sugar or plain granulated sugar**
½ **teaspoon cinnamon**
1 (17.5 ounce) package (2 sheets) frozen puff pastry, thawed
1 egg, lightly beaten

Preheat oven to 350°.

In small bowl, combine sugar and cinnamon and stir well to mix. Set aside.

Unroll 1 thawed puff pastry sheet and roll out to rectangle about 12 x 18 inches.

Brush egg lightly over entire surface and sprinkle with about ⅓ sugar mixture.

Bring long edges of pastry to meet in middle, leaving about ¼-inch space between edges along the "spine". Gently flatten pastry with your hands.

Brush pastry with egg and sprinkle more sugar. Bring edges together to meet in middle and again flatten pastry gently with hands.

Brush egg over pastry strip and sprinkle with sugar. (Half the sugar mixture should be gone.) Fold 1 side of pastry over to join other side. Lightly dust each side with sugar.

Wrap tightly and freeze while you repeat previous steps with other pastry sheet.

Unwrap pastry roll and use very sharp knife to cut pastry into ½-inch slices.

(continued on next page)

(continued)

Place each slice flat side down on lightly greased baking sheet about 2 inches apart.

Bake for 12 minutes and turn each palmier over using thin turner.

Bake for another 5 or 7 minutes until palmiers are golden brown.

Remove from oven and cool on rack. Serve as accompaniment to ice cream or simply by themselves.

Turbinado sugar

Turbinado sugar is raw sugar that has been steam cleaned to remove contaminates. It still retains some molasses, which gives it a golden-brown or amber color. The cleaning also removes enough "stickiness" to allow sugar to flow freely. This sugar has a slightly larger crystal than refined white sugar.

Palmiers

Pronounced "pahlm-YAY" and also called "palm leaves" because of their resemblance to the plant, these crispy, delicate cookies are made from sheets of folded puff pastry that are sprinkled with sugar and baked until the sugar caramelizes. They are delicious with coffee, tea or as accompaniments to other desserts.

The light tender pastry used for these is made from many layers of dough and butter that has been folded and re-rolled several times. As the pastry bakes, the moisture in the butter creates steam, causing the dough to puff and separate into hundreds of flaky layers.

Although very easy to work with, there are a few things to keep in mind when using puff pastry.

- Remove as many pastry sheets as needed. (Wrap unused sheets in plastic wrap or foil and return them to the freezer.)

- For a quick thaw, separate the pastry sheets and cover each one with a piece of plastic wrap. Thaw the sheets at room temperature about 30 minutes.

- Work with 1 pastry sheet at a time and keep the others in refrigerator.

- Unfold pastry sheets on a lightly floured board, countertop or pastry cloth. If pastry becomes too soft, chill for a few minutes.

- Handle pastry as little as possible to ensure tenderness. Cut pastry with sharp knife.

Coconut Rounds

½ cup (1 stick) butter or margarine
1 (6 ounce) can frozen orange juice concentrate, thawed
1 box powdered sugar
1 cup pecans
1 (12 ounce) box vanilla wafers, crushed

Cream butter. Add orange juice concentrate, sugar and pecans and mix well.

Stir in vanilla wafers and add to orange mixture. Mix well.

Form mixture into balls 1½ inches in diameter. Roll balls in coconut.

Let set before storing.

Snowballs

1 cup semi-sweet chocolate chips
⅓ cup evaporated milk
1¼ cups powdered sugar
½ cup chopped walnuts
1⅓ cups flaked coconut

Combine chocolate and milk in medium saucepan.

Cook and stir over low heat until chocolate melts and mixture is smooth.

Remove from heat and stir in powdered sugar and walnuts.

Cool mixture slightly and shape into 1-inch balls. Roll balls in coconut.

Bourbon Balls

½ cup butter, softened
1 (1 pound) box powdered sugar
½ cup bourbon
2 cups finely chopped pecans
4 ounces sweet chocolate

In medium bowl, cream butter and sugar. Add bourbon a little at a time, mixing well after each addition.

Stir in pecans. Chill until dough is well chilled, about 2 hours, and firm enough to shape into 1½-inch balls.

Place balls on baking sheet lined with wax paper or aluminum foil. Chill several hours or overnight.

Melt chocolate in top of double boiler or in small saucepan over very low heat. Remove from heat and cool slightly.

Lower each ball into chocolate mixture with slotted spoon. Lift up and let excess chocolate drip off. Place on foil-lined baking sheet to set.

Pecan Balls

1 cup (2 sticks) butter or margarine, softened
4 tablespoons sugar
2 cups flour
2 cups chopped pecans
1 (16 ounce) box powdered sugar

Preheat oven to 300°.

Cream butter and sugar until light and fluffy.

Stir in flour and pecans.

Roll dough into 1-inch balls and place 2 inches apart on ungreased baking sheet.

Bake for 30 to 45 minutes or until lightly browned.

Remove from oven and transfer cookies to cooling rack. When cool, roll twice in powdered sugar.

Hello Dollies

1½ cups graham cracker crumbs
1 (6 ounce) package chocolate chips
1 cup flaked coconut
1¼ cups chopped pecans
1 (14 ounce) can sweetened condensed milk

Sprinkle cracker crumbs in 9 x 9-inch pan.

Layer chocolate chips, coconut and pecans in pan.

Pour condensed milk over top of layered ingredients.

Bake at 350° for 25 to 30 minutes. Cool and cut into squares.

Rainbow Cookie Ribbons

White chocolate bits taste great in this too!

½ cup (1 stick) margarine
2 cups graham cracker crumbs
1 (14 ounce) can sweetened condensed milk
⅔ cup flaked coconut
1 cup chopped pecans
1 cup **M & M's** plain chocolate candies

Melt margarine in oven in 9 x 13-inch baking pan.

Sprinkle crumbs over margarine and pour condensed milk over crumbs.

Top with coconut, pecans and chocolate candies. Press down to even out.

Bake at 350° for 25 to 30 minutes or until lightly browned.   Cool and cut into bars.

Lemon Cloud Bars

1 (1 pound) package 1-step angel food cake mix
1 (20 ounce) can lemon pie filling
⅓ cup margarine, softened
2 cups powdered sugar
2 tablespoons lemon juice

Combine cake mix and lemon pie filling and stir until well mixed.

Pour into greased, floured 9 x 13-inch baking pan.

Bake at 350° for 25 minutes.

Just before cake is done, mix margarine, powdered sugar and lemon juice together and spread over hot cake.

When cool, cut into bars. Store in refrigerator.

Easy Nutty Bars

4 eggs
1 (14 ounce) box brown sugar
2 tablespoons butter or margarine
2 cups self-rising flour
1 cup nuts

Preheat oven to 350°.

Beat eggs and add sugar and butter. Place in medium saucepan over low heat and cook until sugar and butter melt.

Remove from heat and add flour and nuts.

Bake for 25 to 30 minutes. Cool and cut into bars.

Creamy Pecan Squares

1 (18 ounce) box yellow cake mix
3 eggs, divided
½ cup (1 stick) margarine, softened
2 cups chopped pecans
1 (8 ounce) package cream cheese, softened
3⅔ cups powdered sugar

In mixing bowl, combine cake mix, 1 egg and margarine.

Stir in pecans and mix well.

Press into greased 9 x 13-inch baking pan.

In mixing bowl, beat cream cheese, sugar and remaining eggs until smooth. Pour over pecan mixture.

Bake at 350° for 55 minutes or until golden brown.

Cool and cut into squares.

Crispy Peanut Butter Bars

A quick tasty treat that is great for taking to functions or using for a bake sale. The bars stay crispy and are fairly neat to eat and easy to wrap. For a special treat, cover in chocolate before cutting into bars.

3 tablespoons butter or margarine
4 cups miniature marshmallows
½ cup peanut butter
6 cups crisped rice cereal

Melt butter in medium saucepan over low heat.

Add marshmallows and stir until marshmallows melt. Remove from heat.

Stir peanut butter into marshmallow mixture, stiffing until smooth.

Add cereal and quickly stir until well coated.

Press mixture into buttered 9x13-inch baking pan and cool. Cut into bars.

Optional: Consider chocolate-coated bars. Melt 2 cups semi-sweet or milk chocolate chips and heat to lukewarm. Spread chocolate over bars and let set. Cut and serve.

Easy Blonde Brownies

**1 (1 pound) box light brown sugar
4 eggs
2 cups biscuit mix
2 cups chopped pecans**

Preheat oven to 350°.

In mixing bowl beat together brown sugar, eggs and biscuit mix.

Stir in pecans and pour into greased 9 x 13-inch baking dish.

Bake for 35 minutes.

Cool and cut into squares.

Everyday Special Brownies

1 cup butter
1½ cups dark chocolate pieces
3 eggs
1¼ cups sugar
1 cup flour

Preheat oven to 350°.

Melt butter and chocolate in double boiler over low heat. Cool to room temperature.

Beat eggs to foamy in medium bowl. Stir in sugar and beat at medium speed for 2 to 3 minutes.

Reduce speed and slowly pour in chocolate-butter mixture.

Slowly pour in flour a little at a time.

Pour into greased, floured 9 x 13-inch baking pan.

Bake for 35 to 45 minutes or until brownies are done in middle.

Cool and cut into squares.

German Chocolate Brownie Bars

1 (14 ounce) package caramels, unwrapped
1 (12 ounce) can evaporated milk, divided
1 (18.25 ounce) box chocolate cake mix
1 cup chopped pecans
1 cup semi-sweet chocolate chips

Preheat oven to 350°.

Combine caramels with ⅓ cup evaporated milk in top of double boiler set on low heat over simmering water.

Stir until caramels melt and mixture is smooth. Remove from heat and set aside.

In large bowl, combine cake mix with pecans and remaining evaporated milk.

Spread half of batter in bottom of greased 9 x 13-inch baking pan.

Bake for 6 minutes. Remove from oven and sprinkle with chocolate chips, then drizzle caramel mixture evenly over top.

Drop remaining half of batter by spoonful over caramel mixture.

Bake 15 to 20 minutes more. Remove from oven and cool before cutting.

Easy Gooey Turtle Bars

½ cup (1 stick) margarine, melted
2 cups vanilla wafer crumbs
1 (12 ounce) semi-sweet chocolate morsels
1 cup pecan pieces
1 (12 ounce) jar caramel topping

Combine margarine and wafer crumbs in 9 x 13-inch baking pan and press into bottom of pan.

Sprinkle with chocolate morsels and pecans.

Remove lid from caramel topping and microwave on HIGH for ½ minute or until hot. Drizzle over pecans.

Bake at 350° for about 10 to 15 minutes or until morsels melt and cool in pan.

Chill at least 30 minutes before cutting into squares.

Tip: Make sure chocolate morsels melt, but crumbs don't burn.

Crispy Chocolate Bars

1 (20 ounce) package chocolate-flavored candy-coating squares
¾ cup light corn syrup
¼ cup (½ stick) margarine
2 teaspoons vanilla
8 cups crispy rice cereal

Combine chocolate, corn syrup and margarine in double boiler.

Heat on low, stirring occasionally, until coating melts. Remove from heat and stir in vanilla.

Place cereal in large mixing bowl, pour chocolate mixture over top and stir until well mixed.

Quickly spoon mixture into buttered 9 x 13-inch dish and press down using back of spoon.

Allow to cool and cut into bars.

Caramel-Chocolate Bars

1 (18 ounce) box caramel cake mix
2 eggs
⅓ cup firmly packed light brown sugar
¼ cup (½ stick) margarine, softened
1 cup semi-sweet chocolate chips

Combine cake mix, eggs, ¼ cup water, brown sugar and margarine in large bowl.

Stir until thoroughly blended. (Mixture will be thick.)

Stir in chocolate chips. Spread in greased, floured 9 x 13-inch baking pan.

Bake at 350° for about 25 to 30 minutes or until toothpick inserted in center comes out clean.

Cool before cutting.

Rocky Road Bars

1 (12 ounce) package semi-sweet chocolate morsels
1 (14 ounce) can sweetened condensed milk
2 tablespoons margarine
2 cups dry-roasted peanuts
1 (10 ounce) package miniature marshmallows

Place chocolate morsels, milk and margarine in double boiler and heat on low.

Stir constantly until chocolate melts.

Remove from heat and stir in peanuts and marshmallows.

Spread mixture quickly onto wax paper-lined 9 x 13 inch pan. Chill at least 2 hours.

Cut into bars and store in refrigerator.

Cream Cheese-Strawberry Bars

1 (18.25 ounce) strawberry cake mix
1/2 (1 stick) cup butter or margarine
3 eggs, divided
1 (8 ounce) package cream cheese, softened
2 cups powdered sugar

Preheat oven to 325°.

In large bowl combine cake mix, butter and 1 egg and blend well.

Press mixture into bottom of greased 9 x 13-inch baking dish.

In medium bowl, mix cream cheese, 2 eggs and sugar until mixture is smooth.

Pour mixture over cake batter and bake for 30 to 35 minutes or until lightly browned.

Buttery Walnut Squares

1 cup (2 sticks) butter, softened
1¾ cups packed brown sugar
1¾ cups flour

Cream together butter and sugar.

Add flour and mix well.

Pat mixture evenly in greased 9 x 13-inch baking dish.

Bake at 350° for 15 minutes.

Topping:

1 cup packed brown sugar
4 eggs, lightly beaten
2 tablespoons flour
2 cups chopped walnuts
1 cup flaked coconut

In mixing bowl combine sugar and eggs. Add flour and mix well.

Fold in walnuts and coconut and pour over crust.

Bake at 350° for 20 to 25 minutes or just until center is set.

Cool in pan and cut into squares.

Optional: Top with a scoop of vanilla ice cream.

Caramel Treats

24 chocolate graham crackers squares
1 cup (2 sticks) butter
1 cup firmly packed brown sugar
1½ cups chopped pecans

Preheat oven to 350°.

Place graham cracker squares (do not separate) in single layer in bottom of greased jelly-roll pan or baking sheet with rim.

In medium saucepan, combine butter and brown sugar and bring to boil.

Simmer for 2 minutes stirring constantly or until mixture starts to thicken.

Remove from heat and immediately pour evenly over graham crackers.

Sprinkle nuts evenly on top.

Bake for 15 minutes. Remove from oven and cool.

Nutty Orange Logs

1 (12 ounce) box vanilla wafers, crushed
½ cup (1 stick) margarine, melted
1 (16 ounce) box powdered sugar
1 (6 ounce) can frozen orange juice, undiluted
1 cup finely chopped pecans

Combine wafers, margarine, sugar and orange juice and mix well.

Form into balls and roll in chopped pecans. Store in airtight container.

Sticky Cinnamon Rolls

1½ cups firmly packed brown sugar, divided
1 cup (2 sticks) butter or margarine, softened, divided
1 cup chopped walnuts, divided
1 loaf frozen bread dough, thawed
1 tablespoon ground cinnamon

Butter 9 x 13-inch baking dish. Bring 1 cup brown sugar and ½ cup butter to boil in heavy small saucepan.

Boil for 1 minute. Remove from heat and stir in ½ cup walnuts. Pour into prepared dish.

Roll dough out on lightly floured surface to 15 x 9-inch rectangle. Spread dough evenly with remaining ½ cup butter.

Sprinkle with remaining ½ cup brown sugar and 1 tablespoon cinnamon.

Sprinkle with remaining ½ cup walnuts.

Roll up jelly-roll style, starting at one long side. Slice dough into 1-inch thick rounds.

Arrange dough slices cut side down in prepared dish and space out evenly. Cover with plastic.

Let rise in warm, draft-free area until doubled, about 45 minutes.

Preheat oven to 350°.

Bake rolls until golden brown, about 25 minutes. Let stand 5 minutes.

Turn out onto platter. Cool slightly and serve warm.

Optional: Add ½ cup raisins when you sprinkle dough with walnuts.

Quick Sticky Buns

**1 (3.75 ounce) package regular butterscotch pudding mix
1 cup chopped pecans
½ cup packed brown sugar
¼ cup (½ stick) butter or margarine, softened
1 or 2 packages frozen rolls, thawed**

Combine pudding mix, nuts, sugar and butter in bowl and stir until crumbly.

Use enough frozen rolls to equal 32 pieces of dough.

Sprinkle ¼ of topping into each of 2 greased (9 x 5-inch) loaf pans.

Arrange 16 pieces of dough in each.

Sprinkle with half the remaining topping. Cover and let rise in warm place until almost double, about 1 hour.

Bake at 350° for 35 to 40 minutes. Turn out of pans immediately.

Optional: Add 1 teaspoon cinnamon to dry mixture before sprinkling in pan.

Chocolate-Covered Strawberries

2 - 3 pints fresh strawberries with stems
1 (12 ounce) package semi-sweet chocolate chips
2 tablespoons shortening

Make sure strawberries are clean and dry.

In small, heavy saucepan over low heat, melt chocolate chips and shortening, stirring constantly until mixture is mixed and smooth.

Cool slightly. Hold strawberries by top and dip ⅔ of each strawberry into chocolate mixture.

Over saucepan, drip excess chocolate off strawberry.

Place on tray covered with wax paper. After all berries have been dipped, chill about 1 hour or until chocolate is set and firm.

Remove from tray, cover and chill under ready to serve.

Crunchy Pecan Bites

1 (12 ounce) package milk chocolate chips
¾ cup chopped salted or unsalted pecans
½ cup (1 stick) butter, softened
½ cup sugar
2 tablespoons light corn syrup

Line 9-inch square pan with aluminum foil and coat with non-stick spray.

In heavy saucepan over medium heat, melt butter and stir in corn syrup and sugar. Stir constantly until sugar dissolves.

Pour in pecans and stir until mixture begins to thicken and turn golden brown.

Pour chocolate chips evenly over bottom of baking pan. Pour butter mixture over chocolate chips and spread evenly.

Cool several hours to set or chill in refrigerator. Use foil to lift from pan and break into pieces.

Stained Glass Fudge

1 (12 ounce) package (2 cups) chocolate chips
½ cup (1 stick) butter or margarine
1 cup coarsely chopped pecans or walnuts
1 (10.5 ounce) bag miniature colored marshmallows
½ cup flaked coconut

Melt chocolate and butter in top of double boiler over simmering water stir until mixture is smooth. Remove from heat and cool slightly.

Stir in nuts and marshmallows.

Divide mixture in half and shape each into log about 2 inches wide.

Roll each log in coconut, then wrap in plastic wrap or foil.

Chill for several hours or overnight.

Slice each log into pieces about ⅓-inch thick.

Quick Chocolate Bites

This is a 5-minute answer for unhappy kids.

2 cups semi-sweet or milk chocolate chips
1 tablespoon butter or margarine
½ cup raisins
½ cup chopped pecans, toasted

Combine chocolate chips and butter in top of double boiler set over simmering water and low heat.

Stir frequently until chocolate melts and mixture is smooth.

Remove from heat and stir in raisins and pecans.

Drop by heaping teaspoonfuls onto wax paper or foil. Chill until ready to serve.

Tip: To toast pecans, spread out on baking sheet and cook at 350° for about 5 minutes until nuts are browned slightly.

Easy Fast Fudge

1 (14 ounce) can sweetened condensed milk
3 cups (18 ounces) semi-sweet or milk chocolate chips
Pinch salt
1 teaspoon vanilla

Combine milk, chocolate chips and salt in medium saucepan over medium to low heat.

Stir constantly until chocolate melts.

Remove from heat and stir in vanilla.

Spread in buttered 8 x 8-inch pan and cool.

Snowy Almond Fudge

1 (10 ounce) package premier white chocolate chips
⅔ cup sweetened condensed milk
1½ cups chopped, slivered almonds, toasted
½ teaspoon vanilla extract

Line bottom and sides of 8 x 8-inch baking pan with foil and set aside.

In medium saucepan melt white chocolate chips over very low heat, stirring constantly.

Stir in sweetened condensed milk and mix until well blended and smooth.

Remove from heat and stir in almonds and vanilla. Stir to mix well.

Pour into foil-lined pan and cover.

Chill for several hours until firm. Remove from refrigerator and lift fudge from pan with foil.

Remove foil and cut into squares.

Chocolate-Peanut Clusters

1 cup semi-sweet chocolate chips
½ cup premier white chocolate chips
1 tablespoon shortening
1 (11 ounce) package lightly salted peanuts, divided

Microwave chocolate chips, white chocolate chips and shortening on HIGH for 1 to 2 minutes or until chips melt.

Stir mixture to blend chips and to get smooth texture.

Set aside ¼ cup peanuts for topping.

Pour remaining 2 cups peanuts into mixture and stir to mix well.

Drop by teaspoons into 1-inch clusters onto baking pan or cookie sheet.

Put remaining peanuts on top of each cluster.

Chill uncovered until clusters are firm. Store in airtight container.

Yields about 2 ½ to 3 dozen.

Chocolate Truffles

¾ cup (1½ sticks) butter
¾ cup cocoa
1 (14 ounce) can sweetened condensed milk
3 tablespoons rum
1 cup finely chopped pecans, divided

Melt butter in small saucepan and stir in cocoa until smooth. (Make sure all lumps are gone.)

Stir constantly while slowly pouring in condensed milk.

Continue to stir and cook mixture, about 5 minutes, until it thickens and turns smooth and shiny.

Remove from heat and stir in rum and ¾ cup pecans.

Pour into baking pan and chill for several hours until firm enough to shape into balls.

Remove mixture from pan by tablespoon and shape into 1-inch balls.

Roll in remaining chopped pecans and put on plate to chill several more hours before serving.

Nut Truffles

8 ounces semi-sweet chocolate, chopped
½ cup plus 2 tablespoons whipping cream
1 tablespoon brandy
6 tablespoons ground toasted pecans
⅓ cup cocoa powder

Place chocolate in medium bowl. Bring cream to simmer in small saucepan.

Pour over chocolate. Let stand for 2 minutes.

Whisk until smooth and mix in brandy. Cool completely, stirring occasionally, about 30 minutes.

Use a mixer to beat chocolate mixture until fluffy and lighter in color, about 4 minutes. Mix in pecans.

Cover and chill mixture until firm, about 2 hours.

Line baking sheet with wax paper. Place cocoa powder in another bowl.

Use hands or melon baller to shape chocolate into balls about 1 inch wide. Roll each ball in cocoa to coat.

Cover and chill until firm.

Dates

Dates grow in clusters on date palm trees, which are native to the Middle East and are the oldest known cultivated plant. Date palms can reach heights of 100 feet. Each tree usually contains from 12 to 15 date clusters, which can weigh 20 pounds each and contain up to 200 dates.

The Medjool variety used in this recipe has been called the "fruit of kings" for its outstanding qualities: soft, tender skin, moist texture and delicious flavor. Plump in appearance and averaging over 2 inches in length, these dates are incredibly sweet naturally.

Dates are a fresh fruit. They can be stored at room temperature for up to 2 months, in the refrigerator for up to one year or in the freezer for several years.

Chocolate-Dipped Stuffed Dates

Although it sometimes seems that adding anything at all to these luscious dates is "gilding the lily", (because they are fabulous just by themselves), this is a truly exquisite treat with the addition of nuts and chocolate. This date recipe makes a great finger food, because it is easy and neat to eat.

24 Medjool dates
24 walnut halves
3 ounces semi-sweet chocolate, melted

Use a paring knife to slice each date on one side and remove pit. Insert walnut half.

Dip each stuffed date halfway in melted chocolate and place on wax paper or foil to set.

Tip: If you cut from one end of the date toward the stem end, the pit may be easily pushed out by the knife as you slice.

Pecan Toffee

This delightful candy is very easy to make.

1 cup (2 sticks) plus 2 tablespoons butter
1 cup firmly packed brown sugar
1 cup coarsely chopped pecans
2 (3.5 ounce) premium dark or milk chocolate bars

Use 2 tablespoons butter to grease 9 x 13-inch baking dish and large saucepan.

Place remaining 1 cup butter in saucepan and melt over medium high heat.

Stir in brown sugar and bring to a boil.

Boil sugar mixture for 12 minutes, stirring constantly and occasionally washing down sides of pan with wet pastry brush.

Remove pan from heat and quickly stir in pecans.

Pour toffee mixture into greased baking pan and use buttered spatula to spread evenly.

Place chocolate bars on top of toffee and melt.

When melted, spread chocolate evenly over surface.

Let cool and cut into pieces.

(continued on next page)

(continued)

Tips: When making candy, it is imperative to avoid sugar crystals contaminating the entire batch and becoming too sugary. It is necessary to grease sides of pan with butter before starting and to wash down the sides of the pan with a pastry brush during preparation.

I keep a small glass of water near the stove with the pastry brush in it and occasionally brush the inside of the pan, dipping the brush back in the water as needed. This dissolves the sugar crystals, keeping them from contaminating the mixture. Don't worry about the water dripping down into the candy. It evaporates as the mixture cooks.

Another tip to avoid "sugary" candy is not to scrape the bottom of the pan when pouring the toffee mixture into the baking dish.

Almond-Butter Toffee

1 cup sugar
1 cup butter
1 (6 ounce) package semi-sweet chocolate
¼ cup sliced almonds

In a medium saucepan over medium heat, met sugar and butter, stirring frequently.

Cook about 25 to 30 minutes or until candy thermometer reaches 300°. (If no candy thermometer is available, pour several drops into ice water. If brittle strands form, candy is ready.)

Pour into wax paper-lined, large baking pan and spread to about ¼-inch thickness.

Sprinkle chocolate chips over candy and spread evenly. Let stand for at least 5 minutes.

Sprinkle with almonds and press down lightly.

Cool thoroughly and break into pieces.

Walnut Maples

This is a take-off of the favorite peanut brittle. It is really a nice change.

1 cup packed brown sugar
¾ cup maple syrup
¼ cup butter
1 cup salted walnuts
½ teaspoon baking soda

In medium saucepan over medium heat, stir brown sugar and syrup together until sugar dissolves. Stir frequently so sugar will not burn.

Bring sugar-syrup mixture to boil and continue to stir, about 5 to 8 minutes.

Add butter to mixture and continue cooking, about 15 minutes, until temperature on candy thermometer reaches 300°.

Remove from heat and stir in walnuts and baking soda.

Pour mixture onto large buttered, baking sheet and spread to about ¼-inch thickness.

Cool completely and break into pieces.

Tip: If you do not have a candy thermometer, pour a few drops of sugar-syrup-butter mixture into ice water. If a hard brittle strand forms, candy is ready for cashews and baking soda.

Creole Pralines

3 cups sugar
1 cup water
1 teaspoon vinegar
1 tablespoon butter
3 cups chopped pecans

Combine sugar, water and vinegar. Cook to soft-ball stage or when candy thermometer reaches 236°.

Stir in butter and pecans.

Remove from heat and beat until mixture thickens slightly.

Drop by teaspoon onto wax paper. Cool completely.

Cashew Crunch

1 cup sugar
1 cup (2 sticks) butter
1 tablespoon light corn syrup
1½ cups salted cashew pieces

In medium saucepan over medium heat, melt sugar, butter and corn syrup, stirring frequently.

Cook for about 25 to 30 minutes or until candy thermometer reaches 300°. (If no candy thermometer is available, pour several drops into ice water. If brittle strands form, candy is ready.)

Pour into wax paper-lined, large baking pan and spread to about ¼-inch thickness.

Sprinkle cashew pieces over top and press down lightly.

Cool thoroughly and break into pieces.

Almond Caramels

12 (15x1½ inch) graham crackers
¾ cup packed brown sugar
¾ cup butter
1 (6 ounce) package premium, semi-sweet chocolate chips
1 cup slivered almonds

Lay graham crackers in bottom of foil-lined, (15x10 inch) jellyroll pan.

In medium saucepan over medium heat, melt butter and brown sugar, stirring frequently, until sugar dissolves.

Bring sugar mixture to full boil and stir continuously for about 5 minutes.

Pour mixture over graham crackers and spread mixture to coat crackers.

Pour chocolate chips over and let stand for 1 minute. Spread chocolate chips in swirling motion.

Sprinkle almond slivers over chocolate and press into chocolate to hold almonds.

Cool thoroughly and break into pieces.

Microwave Pecan Brittle

This candy is so easy and it does not require a candy thermometer!

1 cup sugar
½ cup light corn syrup
1 cup pecan halves or pieces
1 teaspoon butter
1 teaspoon baking soda

Put sugar and corn syrup in large microwave-safe bowl. Microwave on HIGH for 4 minutes.

Stir in pecans and cook on HIGH for another 4 minutes.

Stir in butter and mix well. Cook for 2 minutes.

Add baking soda and stir until foamy.

Grease baking sheet or shallow-rimmed baking pan.

Spread mixture on sheet or in pan and let cool for 30 minutes. Break into pieces.

Tip: For additional flavor, you may add ¼ teaspoon cinnamon with the sugar and corn syrup and 1 teaspoon vanilla with the butter.

Coconut Sweets

½ cups powdered sugar
2 cups flaked coconut
½ cup cold mashed potatoes
1 teaspoon almond extract
½ teaspoon vanilla

In large mixing bowl combine powdered sugar, coconut, mashed potatoes, almond extract and vanilla.

Beat at low speed for several minutes and scrap the bowl to mix thoroughly.

Press coconut mixture onto wax paper-lined, large baking pan and roll flat with rolling pin. Cover and freeze 1 hour.

Lightly coat flat surface with powdered sugar.

Lift wax paper from pan and turn it over onto coated, flat surface.

Use cookie cutters to cut-out candy shapes or roll into 1-inch balls.

Optional: Decorate with candy sprinkles, candy coating or frosting.

Easy Chocolate Dessert Fondue

1 (12 ounce) package semi-sweet chocolate chips
¾ cup half-and-half
½ cup sugar
Strawberries, mandarin orange sections, cherries, bananas

In heavy saucepan melt chocolate chips, half-and-half and sugar over medium heat, stirring constantly, until chocolate melts and mixture is well blended.

Pour into fondue pot and serve.

Makes about 2 cups.

Cakes

Mom's Pound Cake

1 cup (2 sticks) butter, softened
2 cups sugar
5 eggs
2 cups flour
1 tablespoon almond flavoring

Combine all ingredients in mixing bowl and beat for 10 minutes at median speed.

Pour into greased and floured tube pan. (Batter will be very thick.)

Bake at 325° for 1 hour. Test with toothpick for doneness.

Old Southern Praline Sauce

Pour this sauce over Mom's Pound Cake
and you just may see Scarlet coming up the drive.

2 eggs
1 (1 pound) box light brown sugar
2 tablespoons flour
½ cup (1 stick) butter
1 teaspoon vanilla
1½ cups chopped pecans

Beat eggs and combine with brown sugar and flour to mix.

In skillet melt butter and stir in brown sugar mixture, stirring constantly.

Remove from heat and stir in vanilla and pecans.

Spread praline sauce over top of cake.

Pound Cake A La Blueberries

1 (18 ounce) box yellow cake mix
1 (8 ounce) package cream cheese, softened
½ cup oil
4 eggs
1 (15 ounce) can whole blueberries, drained

With mixer, combine cake mix, cream cheese, oil and eggs and beat for 3 minutes.

Stir in blueberries and mix well.

Pour into greased, floured bundt or tube pan.

Bake at 350° for 50 minutes. Test with toothpick to be sure cake is done.

Sprinkle powdered sugar over top of cake, if desired.

Fancy Pound Cake

1 bakery pound cake
1 (15 ounce) can crushed pineapple, undrained
1 (3.4 ounce) package coconut instant pudding mix
1 (8 ounce) carton whipped topping
½ cup flaked coconut

Slice cake horizontally to make 3 layers

Mix pineapple, pudding and whipped topping together and blend well.

Spread on each layer and sprinkle top of cake with coconut.

Chill before serving.

Lemon Pound Cake

2 cups sugar
1 (2 sticks) butter or margarine
6 eggs
2 cups flour
1 teaspoon lemon extract

Preheat oven at 350°.

Cream sugar and butter until light and fluffy.

Add eggs, one at a time, beating well after each addition.

Gradually add flour and lemon extract.

Pour batter into greased loaf pan and bake for 50 to 60 minutes. Cake is done with toothpick or cake tester is inserted in center and comes out clean.

Serve with Raspberry Sauce (page 11) spooned over each slice.

Lemony Sponge Cake

1 (18 ounce) box yellow cake mix
4 eggs
½ cup plus 2 tablespoons vegetable oil
3 teaspoons lemon extract
⅔ cup apricot nectar

Preheat oven to 350°.

In small bowl crack eggs and beat slightly to mix.

In large bowl combine yellow cake mix and eggs until eggs are absorbed into mixture.

Pour in oil, lemon extract and apricot nectar and mix well.

Pour cake mixture into greased, floured cake pan.

Bake for 40 to 45 minutes.

Optional: A lemon glaze is wonderful poured over the top of this cake. Mix the juice of 2 lemons and 1 ½ cups powdered sugar until smooth and pour over the top of cake after it has cooled slightly.

Creamy Sunshine Cake

**1 (18 ounce) box butter cake mix
½ cup (1 stick) butter, melted
4 eggs, divided
1 (16 ounce) box powdered sugar, divided
1 (8 ounce) package cream cheese, softened**

In mixing bowl, beat together cake mix with butter and 2 eggs.

Spread mixture into greased and floured 9 x 13-inch baking pan.

Set aside ¾ cup powdered sugar and mix remaining powdered sugar with remaining 2 eggs and cream cheese. Beat until smooth.

Spread mixture on top of dough. Sprinkle remaining powdered sugar on top.

Bake cake at 350° for 40 minutes. Cake will puff up and then go down when cake is cooled.

Layered Strawberry-Lemon Cake

¾ cup milk
1 (7 ounce) jar marshmallow creme
2 (8 ounce) cartons lemon yogurt
1 (10 ounce) pound cake
1 pint strawberries, sliced, sugared

In large bowl, add milk slowly to marshmallow creme while beating on low speed. When blended and smooth, stir in yogurt and set aside.

Slice pound cake horizontally to make 3 layers.

Place ⅓ yogurt mixture in 9 x 5-inch loaf pan. Place 1 pound cake layer on top. (The pound cake will probably be smaller in diameter than the loaf pan, so just center it the best you can).

Place another ⅓ yogurt mixture over cake slice and top with second cake layer.

Pour remaining yogurt mixture on top and add third cake layer. (Because getting third cake layer on top is such a tight squeeze, I slice it into thinner layers and cover entire top with cake to the edges of pan. This cake layer serves as base and needs to cover entire width of pan).

Spread strawberries over top.

Cover with plastic wrap and place in freezer until firm.

Cut around edges of pan with knife.

Put plate on top of pan and invert to remove cake from pan.

Warm knife with hot water before slicing.

Golden Butter Cake

1 cup (2 sticks) butter
2 cups sugar
3 eggs
2 cups flour
2 tablespoons orange juice

Preheat oven to 350°.

Cream sugar and butter until light and fluffy.

Add eggs one at a time and beat after each addition.

Stir in flour and orange juice.

Pour into greased, floured bundt cake or tube cake pan.

Bake for about 1 hour. Cake is done with toothpick or cake tester is inserted in center and comes out clean.

Chocolate-Cherry Cake

1 (18 ounce) milk chocolate cake mix
1 (20 ounce) cherry pie filling
3 eggs

Preheat oven to 350°.

Combine cake mix, pie filling and eggs in mixing bowl and mix by hand.

Pour into greased, floured 9 x 13-inch baking pan.

Bake for 35 to 40 minutes. Test cake for doneness with toothpick.

Frosting

5 tablespoons margarine
1¼ cups sugar
½ cup milk
1 (6 ounce) package chocolate chips

Combine margarine, sugar and milk in medium saucepan.

Bring to boil and cook for 1 minute stirring constantly.

Add chocolate chips and stir until chips melt.

Pour over hot cake.

Super Oreo Cake

1 (18½ ounce) package white cake mix
1¼ cups water
⅓ cup oil
4 egg whites
1¼ cups coarsely crushed Oreo cookies

Grease and flour 2 (8 or 9 inch) round cake pans and set aside.

Preheat oven at 350°.

In large mixing bowl, combine cake mix, water, oil and egg whites and blend on slow speed until moistened.

Beat 2 minutes on high speed.

Gently fold in coarsely crushed cookies. Pour batter into prepared pans.

Bake for 25 to 30 minutes or until toothpick inserted in center comes out clean.

Cool 10 minutes and remove form pan. Cool completely.

Frosting:

4¼ cups powdered sugar
1 cup (2 sticks) butter, softened
1 cup shortening
1 teaspoon almond flavoring
½ cup crushed Oreo cookies

Beat together with mixer all ingredients except crushed cookie pieces.

Spread frosting on first layer of cake and put second layer on top.

Spread frosting over top layer.

Sprinkle crushed Oreo cookies on top.

Optional: About ¾ cup chopped pecans are great sprinkled over top of cake.

Flourless Chocolate Cake

A very dense, smooth cake, this dessert tastes great by itself or it may be served with ice cream or a vanilla sauce. Its versatility and easy preparation makes it a good standby for all occasions.

7 tablespoons lightly salted butter, divided
9 (1 ounce) squares semi-sweet baking chocolate
7 eggs, separated
⅓ cup sugar
1 cup whipping cream, whipped

Preheat oven at 250°.

Grease 8 x 13-inch round cake pan or springform pan with 1 tablespoon butter.

Coat pan with cocoa instead of flour and set aside.

Combine chocolate and remaining butter in top of double boiler over simmering water.

Cook and stir until chocolate melts and mixture is smooth. Remove from heat.

Mix egg yolks in small bowl. Add small amount of warm chocolate mixture to eggs and stir well.

Stir egg mixture into remaining chocolate and mix well. Set aside.

In large bowl, beat egg whites until soft peaks form.

While beating, add sugar a little at a time until stiff peaks form and mixture is glossy.

(continued on next page)

(continued)

Pour chocolate mixture over egg whites and gently fold in.

Pour batter into prepared pan and bake 50 to 55 minutes. The center should be set, but will wiggle slightly.

Remove from oven and set pan on cooling rack for 10 minutes. If using a springform pan, remove sides of pan. If using one-piece cake pan, invert cake onto serving plate.

Cool completely and chill for several hours before serving.

Tip: For an extra special touch, spoon some Raspberry Sauce (page 11) over each slice before serving. Raspberry sauce is also available at the grocery store. Powdered sugar over cake is also a nice touch.

Golden Rum Cake

1 (18 ounce) box yellow cake mix with pudding
3 eggs
⅓ cup oil
½ cup rum
1 cup chopped pecans

Mix cake mix, eggs, water, oil and rum in mixing bowl and blend well.

Stir in pecans. Pour into greased and floured 10-inch tube or bundt pan.

Bake at 325° for 1 hour. (If you want a sweeter cake, sprinkle powdered sugar over top of cooled cake.)

Chess Cake

1 (18 ounce) box yellow cake mix
2 eggs
½ cup (1 stick) margarine, softened

Beat together cake mix, eggs and margarine. Press into greased 9 x 13-inch baking pan.

Topping:

2 eggs
1 (8 ounce) package cream cheese, softened
1 (1 pound) box powdered sugar

Beat together 2 eggs, cream cheese and powdered sugar. Pour over cake.

Bake at 350° for 35 minutes.

5-Minute Candy Bar Cake

This easy, layered cake has the flavor of an Almond Joy candy bar. I like to frost only the top of the cake so that you see the layers.

1 (16 ounce) frozen pound cake, defrosted
1 (7 ounce) package flaked coconut
1 (14 ounce) can sweetened condensed milk
½ cup chopped almonds, toasted
1 (16 ounce) carton chocolate fudge frosting

Split pound cake lengthwise into 4 equal layers. (It is easier to slice cake when cake is very cold.)

In small bowl, combine coconut and sweetened condensed milk. Stir until well blended.

Spread half coconut mixture on bottom cake layer. Sprinkle half almonds.

Place second cake layer on top and spread with chocolate frosting.

Repeat layers.

Caramel-Angel Cake

This easy 5-minute recipe will make people think you are an angel!

1 cup packed brown sugar
3 cups whipping cream, chilled
1 (20 ounce) can crushed pineapple, well drained
½ cup ground pecans
1 angel food cake

Mix brown sugar and whipping cream in large bowl and stir well.

Beat whipping cream mixture until peaks form. Gently fold in pineapple and nuts.

Slice angel food cake into 3 layers and spread each layer, sides and top with whipped cream mixture.

Chill 12 to 24 hours before serving.

Creamy Surprise Cake

1 large angel food cake
1 (18 ounce) jar chocolate ice cream topping
½ gallon vanilla ice cream, softened
1 (12 ounce) carton whipped topping
½ cup slivered almonds, toasted

Tear cake into large pieces. Stir in chocolate topping to oat pieces of cake.

Mix in softened ice cream. (Work fast.) Stir into tube pan and freeze overnight.

Turn out onto large cake plate and frost with whipped topping. Decorate with almonds and freeze again before serving.

Old-Fashioned Applesauce Cake

1(18 ounce) box spice cake mix
3 eggs
1¼ cups applesauce
1 cup chopped pecans

With mixing bowl, combine cake mix, eggs, applesauce and oil.

Beat at medium speed for 2 minutes. Stir in pecans.

Pour into 9 x 13-inch greased, floured baking pan.

Bake at 350° for 40 minutes.

Test for doneness with toothpick. Allow to cool.

For frosting, use prepared vanilla frosting and stir in ½ teaspoon cinnamon before spreading on cake.

Fresh Berry Cake

*This is a fun–5 minute recipe because you may use
any combination of berries and fruit.*

**1 angel food cake
⅔ cup strawberry jam, divided
2½ cups fresh blueberries, rinsed, drained, divided
1 pint strawberries, hulled, sliced**

Slice angel food cake in half horizontally.

Place bottom layer on serving plate and spread ⅓ cup jam over. Arrange 1 cup blueberries over jam.

Spread half whipped topping over blueberries within ½ inch of edge of cake.

Place second layer on top and spread remaining jam over. Arrange 1 cup blueberries over jam and spread remaining whipped topping over them.

Arrange strawberry slices and remaining ½ cup blueberries attractively over whipped topping as garnish. Chill until ready to serve.

Cherry-Nut Cake

1(18 ounce) box French vanilla cake mix
½ cup (1 stick) margarine, melted
2 eggs
1 (20 ounce) can cherry pie filling
1 cup chopped pecans

In large bowl, mix all ingredients by hand.

Pour into greased, floured bundt or tube pan.

Bake at 350° for 1 hour. (Sprinkle some powdered sugar on top of cake if you would like a sweeter cake.)

Hawaiian Pineapple Cake

1 (20 ounce) can crushed pineapple, drained
1 (20 ounce) can cherry pie filling
1 (18 ounce) yellow cake mix
1 cup (2 sticks) margarine, softened
1¼ cups chopped pecans

Place all ingredients in large bowl and mix by hand.

Pour into greased and floured 9 x 13-inch baking dish.

Bake at 350° for 1 hour 10 minutes.

Brandy Spiced Peach Cake

1 (20 ounce) peach pie filling
1 (18 ounce) box yellow cake mix
3 eggs
½ cup brandy
¼ cup vegetable oil

In blender, blend pie filling until smooth.

In large bowl, combine pie filling, dry cake mix, eggs, brandy and vegetable oil and blend well.

Pour into greased, floured 9-inch tube pan.

Bake at 350° for 1 hour or until cake springs back when lightly touched.

Optional: Sprinkle with powdered sugar before serving.

Peaches 'n Cream

1 (18 ounce) box yellow cake mix
½ cup butter, melted
3 eggs, divided
1 (20 ounce) can peach pie filling
2 cups sour cream

In large bowl, combine dry cake mix, butter and 2 eggs and blend well.

Pour into 9 x 13-inch baking pan.

Bake at 350° for 25 minutes. Remove from oven.

Spoon pie filling over cake.

In small bowl, combine sour cream and remaining egg.

Pour mixture over pie filling.

Continue baking 15 minutes or until sour cream topping is set.

Cut into 3-inch squares.

Creamy Orange Chiffon Cake
Everyone is surprised at how easy and how good this cake is!

1 bakery orange chiffon cake
1 (15 ounce) can crushed pineapple, undrained
1 (3.4 ounce) package vanilla instant pudding
1 (8 ounce) carton whipped topping
½ cup slivered almonds, toasted

Slice cake horizontally to make 3 layers.

Mix pineapple, pudding and whipped topping together well.

Spread on each layer and then cover top of cake. Sprinkle almonds on top.

Chill before serving.

Deluxe Coconut Cake

1 (18 ounce) package yellow cake mix
1 (14 ounce) can sweetened condensed milk
1 (10 ounce) can cream of coconut
1 (4 ounce) can flaked coconut
1 (8 ounce) carton whipped topping

Prepare yellow cake mix according to directions.

Pour into greased and floured 9 x 13-inch baking pan.

Bake at 350° for 30 to 35 minutes or until toothpick inserted in center comes out clean.

While cake is warm, punch holes in cake about 2 inches apart.

Pour sweetened condensed milk over cake and spread around until all milk has soaked into cake.

Pour coconut cream over cake and sprinkle coconut over top.

Allow to cool, then frost with whipped topping. Chill before serving.

Banana-Butter Cake

1 (18 ounce) box yellow cake mix
2 ripe bananas
3 (2 ounce) Butterfinger candy bars, chopped, divided
½ cut chopped pecans
1 (16 ounce) container prepared white frosting

Preheat oven to 350°.

Prepare cake mix according to package directions.

Mash bananas and stir into cake batter to mix.

Fold in about ¾ cup chopped Butterfinger and chopped nuts.

Pour into greased, floured 9 x 13-inch baking pan.

Bake for 40 to 50 minutes or until toothpick inserted in center comes out clean.

Cool thoroughly before frosting. Remove from pan and spread frosting.

Top with remaining chopped Butterfinger.

Grandma's Strawberry Cake

1 (18 ounce) box strawberry cake mix
1 (3½ ounce) package instant coconut cream pudding mix
⅓ cup oil
4 eggs
1 (3 ounce) package strawberry gelatin

Mix all ingredients plus 1 cup water and beat for 2 minutes at medium speed.

Pour into greased, floured bundt pan.

Bake at 325° for 55 to 60 minutes. Cake is done when toothpick comes out clean.

Cool for 20 minutes before removing cake from pan.

Quick And Easy Fruitcake

1 (15.6 ounce) package cranberry or blueberry quick-bread mix
½ cup chopped pecans
½ cup chopped dates
¼ cup chopped maraschino cherries
¼ cup crushed pineapple, drained

Prepare quick-bread batter according to package directions.

Stir in remaining ingredients. Pour into 9 x 5-inch greased loaf pan.

Bake at 350° for 60 minutes or until a toothpick inserted in cake comes out clean. Cool 10 minutes before removing from pan.

Strawberry-Upside Downs

1 (20 ounce) can strawberry pie filling
½ cup packed light brown sugar
¼ cup (½ stick) butter, melted
1 (18 ounce) box white cake mix

In medium bowl, stir together pie filling, brown sugar and butter until well blended.

Divide filling equally among 8 (10 ounce) custard cups.

Prepare cake mix according to package directions.

Pour over strawberry mixture.

Bake at 350° for 30 minutes or until cake springs back when touched lightly.

Immediately turn out of custard cups. If strawberry mixture adheres to custard cup, spoon over cake.

Poppy Seed Cake

**1 (18 ounce) package yellow cake mix
1 (3.4 ounce) package instant coconut cream pudding mix
½ cup oil
3 eggs
2 tablespoons poppy seeds**

In mixing bowl, combine cake mix and pudding mix, 1 cup water, oil and eggs.

Beat on low speed until moistened. Beat on medium speed for 2 minutes.

Stir in poppy seeds. Pour into greased, floured bundt pan.

Bake at 350° for 50 minutes or until toothpick inserted near the center comes out clean.

Cool for 10 minutes and remove from pan. Dust with powdered sugar.

Pumpkin-Rum Cake

1 (18.25 ounce) white cake mix
1 (15 ounce) can pumpkin
3 eggs
½ cup rum
¾ cup chopped pecans, toasted

Preheat oven at 325°.

In large bowl, combine cake mix, pumpkin, eggs and rum.

Beat on low speed to blend.

Beat on medium speed for 2 minutes.

Fold in pecans.

Pour batter in greased, floured 12-cup bundt cake pan.

Bake for 45 to 50 minutes or until cake tester comes out clean.

Let cool 10 minutes.

Turn out onto serving platter and frost with Orange Glaze.

Orange Glaze:

1 cup powdered sugar
2 tablespoons plus ½ teaspoon orange juice
1 tablespoon orange zest

Mix powdered sugar, orange juice and orange zest until smooth.

Spoon over top of cake allowing glaze to run down sides of cake.

Mini-Pumpkin Cakes

1 (18 ounce) box spice cake mix
1 (15 ounce) can pumpkin
3 eggs
⅓ cup oil
⅓ cup water

In mixing bowl, blend cake mix, pumpkin, eggs, oil and water. Beat for 2 minutes.

Pour batter into 24 paper-lined muffin cups. Fill ¾ full.

Bake at 350° for 18 to 20 minutes or until toothpick inserted in center comes out clean. (If you want a sweeter cupcake, frost with prepared icing.)

Pineapple Upside-Down Cake

½ cup (1 stick) margarine
2 cups packed light brown sugar
1 (20 ounce) can pineapple, crushed, drained
10 maraschino cherries, quartered
1 (18.25 ounce) box pineapple cake mix

Preheat oven to 350°.

In small saucepan melt margarine and brown sugar until creamy.

Divide mixture evenly between 2 (9-inch) cake pans.

Spread crushed pineapple and cherries evenly over brown sugar mixture in each pan.

Prepare cake mix according to package directions and pour over brown sugar-pineapple mixture.

Bake for 35 to 40 minutes or until toothpick inserted in center of cake comes out clean.

Remove cake from oven and cool for 10 minutes.

Put plate on top of cake pan, turn cake pan upside down and tap bottom of cake pan several times with knife. Gently lift cake pan off cake.

Cranberry-Coffee Cake

2 eggs
1 cup mayonnaise
1 (18 ounce) box spice cake mix
1 (16 ounce) can whole cranberry sauce
Powdered sugar

In mixing bowl, beat eggs, mayonnaise and cake mix and mix well. Fold in cranberry sauce.

Pour into greased, floured 9 x 13-inch baking pan.

Bake at 325° for 45 minutes. Test with toothpick to be sure cake is done.

When cake is cool, dust with powdered sugar. (If you would rather have an icing instead of powdered sugar, use a prepared icing.)

Cherry Trifle

1 (12 ounce) pound cake
⅓ cup amaretto
2 (20 ounce) cans cherry pie filling, divided
4 cups vanilla pudding, divided
1 (8 ounce) carton whipped topping

Cut pound cake into ½-inch slices.

Line bottom of 3-quart trifle bowl with cake and brush with amaretto.

Top with 1 cup pie filling and 1 cup pudding. Repeat layers three times.

Top with whipped topping and chill.

Easy Apricot Trifle Express

1 (18 ounce) box yellow cake mix
1 (20 ounce) can apricot pie filling
1 cup sliced almonds, toasted, divided
2 cups whipped topping

Prepare and bake 2 (9-inch) cake layers according to package directions.

Break 1 cake layer into pieces. Freeze remaining cake layer for use later.

Place half of cake pieces into 2-quart serving bowl.

In medium bowl, combine pie filling and ⅔ cup almonds.

Fold in whipped topping.

Spoon half pie filling mixture over cake pieces. Repeat layer of cake pieces and remaining pie filling.

Sprinkle with remaining almonds.

Cover and chill at least 4 hours before serving.

Tortes

Tortes are multi-layered cakes with fillings between layers. Often the cake has little or no flour, but contains breadcrumbs or ground nuts. Today, it is easy to prepare tortes. Buy prepared cakes, slice them horizontally into several layers and prepare fillings that are delicious.

Basic Steps For Making A Torte

A 1-layer cake may be sliced horizontally into 2 pieces or layers for the torte. (A serrated knife slices the best and leaves the fewest crumbs. The cake is easier to cut if it is chilled first.)

Place one layer, cut side down, on a serving plate.

Prepare filling and spread half on top of first layer.

Place second layer, cut side down, over filling. (If there is a slight dome to the last layer, slice off the dome to make it level on top.)

Spread remaining filling over top and garnish with fresh fruit or chocolate curls.

Cherry-Cream Tortes

24 chocolate cookie wafers, crumbled, divided
2 cups (1 pint) sour cream, divided
1 (20 ounce) can cherry pie filling, divided

In each of 8 individual serving dishes, sprinkle about 1 wafer of crumbs in bottom of dish.

Layer 1 tablespoon sour cream on top of crumbs and 1 tablespoon cherry pie filling on top of sour cream.

Repeat with 2 additional layers.

Chill about 1 hour before serving.

Toffee-Meringue Torte

7 egg whites
1¾ cups sugar
1 pint whipping cream, divided
9 chocolate-covered toffee candy bars, crushed or 1 package
almond brickle crisps, divided
1(3.5 - 4 ounce) chocolate bar, shaved

Preheat oven at 350°.

Beat egg whites and sugar to make meringue.

Place in 2 (9-inch) cake pans lined with foil.

Bake for 1 hour. Remove from oven and cool.

Whip cream.

Place one meringue layer on cake plate. Spread half of whipped cream over and sprinkle half of crushed toffee over cream.

Place other meringue layer on top and spread remaining whipped cream over. Sprinkle remaining toffee chips over. Garnish with shaved chocolate.

Chill for several hours before serving.

Easy Creamy Chocolate Torte

1 (10¾ ounce) frozen pound cake
½ cup powdered sugar
¼ cup cocoa
1 cup cold whipping cream
1 teaspoon vanilla extract

Allow cake to thaw and slice horizontally to make 4 layers.

Combine sugar and cocoa in medium bowl. Pour in whipping cream and vanilla and beat until stiff peaks form.

On serving platter, place first layer of cake and spread one-third whipped cream mixture over cake.

Place second layer of cake on top and spread another one-third whipped cream mixture over cake.

Repeat with another cake layer and remaining whipped cream mixture. Top with final slice of cake.

Drizzle chocolate syrup over top and sides or prepare Chocolate Sauce next page.

(continued on next page)

(continued)

Chocolate Sauce:

2 tablespoons butter
2 tablespoons cocoa
2 tablespoons water
1 cup powdered sugar
½ teaspoon almond extract

In small saucepan, melt butter over low heat.

Add cocoa and water, stirring constantly, until mixture is smooth and begins to thicken. Remove from heat.

Slowly pour in powdered sugar and almond extract and mix thoroughly.

Whisk vigorously to remove any lumps and continue to stir until smooth.

Drizzle over top and sides of cake. Chill until ready to serve.

Optional: Sprinkle toasted, slivered almonds over top.

Chocolate-Apricot Torte

Cream cheese gives this cake a different twist. If you aren't crazy about the flavor of cream cheese and jam, simply omit the cheese and layer the cake with jam and frosting.

1 (16 ounce) frozen pound cake, thawed
6 ounces apricot jam or preserves
1 (8 ounce) package Neufchatel or cream cheese, softened
1 (16 ounce) carton chocolate frosting

Slice pound cake lengthwise into 4 equal layers.

Spread some cheese on first layer and top with jam. Put second cake layer on top and frost with chocolate icing.

Repeat layers. Frost sides with chocolate icing.

A

Alcoholic Beverages

Amaretto Pot de Creme au Chocolate 70

Bing Cherry Shortcakes 22

Brandied Cherries 21

Chilled Pumpkin Souffle 83

Cranberry-Chardonnay Sorbet 49

Creamy Chocolate Mousse 74

Creme de Menthe Pie 103

Irish Cream Delight 104

Island-Pineapple Sauce 15

Peachy-Amaretto Crunch 117

Pears Poached in Wine 30

Pina Colada Sorbet 50

Rum Sauce 12

Strawberries Topped with Sweetened Mascarpone 23

Strawberry-Topped Cheesecake 110

Sugared Peaches with Sweet Marsala Wine Sauce 27

Sweet Apricot Alaska 44

Whiskey Cream 14

Wine-Soaked Nectarines 26

Almond Caramels 225

Almond Custard with Chocolate Sauce 62

Almond-Butter Toffee 222

Almond-Meringue Cookies 183

Amaretti 187

Amaretto Pot de Creme au Chocolate 70

Apples

Apple Crisp 118

Apple Dumplings 122

Apple-Spiced Pears 28

Honey-Glazed Apple Turnovers 120

Hot Spiced Apples Topping 14

Lickity-Split Apple Crisp 119

Quick and Easy Apple Pastries 123

Tarte Tatin 133

Apple Crisp 118

Apple Dumplings 122

Apricot

Apricot Cobbler 113

Quick and Easy Apple Pastries 123

Sweet Apricot Alaska 44

Apple-Spiced Pears 28

Apricot Cobbler 113

B

Bananas

Banana Crunch Parfaits 85

Banana-Cream Cheese Pie 100

Cherry Delight 31

Red, White and Gooey Banana Splits 34

Banana Crunch Parfaits 85

Banana-Butter Cake 252

Banana-Cream Cheese Pie 100

Bananas Foster 155

Bars

Buttery Walnut Squares 206

Caramel Treats 207

Caramel-Chocolate Bars 204

Cream Cheese-Strawberry Bars 205

Creamy Pecan Squares 197

Crispy Chocolate Bars 203

Crispy Peanut Butter Bars 198

Easy Blonde Brownies 199

Easy Gooey Turtle Bars 202

Easy Nutty Bars 196

Everyday Special Brownies 200

German Chocolate Brownie Bars 201

Hello Dollies 194

Lemon Cloud Bars 196

Nutty Orange Logs 207

Rainbow Cookie Ribbons 195

Rocky Road Bars 204

Berries

Berry Blue Cobbler 115

Blueberry and Pudding Parfaits 88

Blueberry Hill Crunch 113

Boysenberry Sauce 10

Express Fruit Cobbler 114

Fresh Berry Cake 246

Grandma's Strawberry Cake 253

Lemon Curd Mousse with Blackberry
Sauce 76

Lemon-Raspberry Parfaits 87

Lightning Fast Peach Cobbler 115

Old-Fashion Blueberry Pie 98

Raspberry Sauce 11

Very Merry Berry Pie 95

Berry Blue Cobbler 115

Bing Cherry Shortcakes 22

Blintzes

Cheese Blintzes 149

Black Forest Crepes 153

Black Walnut-Maple Tartlets 144

Blackberry Sauce 76

Blancmange 64

Blueberry and Pudding Parfaits 88

Blueberry Hill Crunch 113

Bourbon Balls 192

Boysenberry Sauce 10

Brandied Cherries 21

Brandied Peach Cake 248

Brown Sugar Cookies 167

Buns

Quick Sticky Buns 209

Sticky Cinnamon Rolls 208

Butter Pecan Cookies 169

Butter Pecan Dreams 168

Butter Pecan-Pumpkin Parfait 43

Butterscotch Haystacks 162

Butterscotch Sweets 163

Buttery Walnut Squares 206

C

Cakes

5-Minute Candy Bar Cake 243

Banana-Butter Cake 252

Brandied Peach Cake 248

Caramel-Angel Cake 244

Cheesy Trifle 260

Cherry-Nut Cake 247

Chocolate-Cherry Cake 238

Cranberry Coffee Cake 259

Creamy Orange Chiffon 250

Creamy Sunshine Cake 235

Deluxe Coconut Cake 251

Easy Apricot Trifle Express 261

Fancy Pound Cake 232

Flourless Chocolate Cake 240

Fresh Berry Cake 246

Golden Butter Cake 237

Golden Rum Cake 242

Grandma's Strawberry Cake 253

Layered Strawberry-Lemon Cake 236

Lemon Pound Cake 233

Lemony Sponge Cake 234

Mini-Pumpkin Cake 257

Mom's Pound Cake 230

Old Fashion Applesauce Cake 245

Old Southern Praline Sauce 230

Peaches N Cream Cake 249

Pineapple Upside-Down Cake 258

Poppy Seed Cake 255

Pound Cake A La Blueberries 231

Pumpkin-Rum Cake 256

Quick And Easy Fruitcake 253

Strawberry-Upside Downs 254

Super Oreo Cake 239

Sweet Apricot Alaska 44

Candied Almond Topping 17

Candies

Almond Caramels 225

Almond-Butter Toffee 222

Cashew Crunch 224

Chocolate Truffles 217

Chocolate-Peanut Clusters 216

Chocolate-Dipped Stuffed Dates 219

Coconut Sweets 227

Easy Chocolate Dessert Fondue 228

Easy Fast Fudge 214

Microwave Pecan Brittle 226

Nut Truffles 218

Pecan Toffee 220

Quick Chocolate Bites 213

Snowy Almond Fudge 215

Stained Glass Fudge 212

Walnut Maples 223

Cantaloupe Sherbet 48

Cappuccino Mousse 79

Caramel Sauce 127

Caramel Sauce 9

Caramel Treats 207

Caramel-Angel Cake 244

Caramel-Chocolate Bars 204

Caramel-Pecan Tarts in Chocolate Shells 140

Cashew Crunch 224

Cenci 128

Charlie McRoons 180

Cheesecakes

Chocolate Cheesecake on Brownie
Crust 111

Crunchy Caramel-Topped Cheesecake
112

Easy Cheesecake 112

Strawberry-Topped Cheesecake 110

Cheeses

Banana-Cream Cheese Pie 100

Chocolate Cheesecake on Brownie
Crust 111

Creamy Peach Parfait Topped With
Almonds 84

Easy Cheesecake 112

Not-So-Sweet Dessert Salad 32

Red, White and Gooey Banana Splits
34

Strawberries Topped with Sweetened
Mascarpone 23

Strawberry-Cream Cheese Pie 90

Strawberry-Fruit Pizza 109

Cheese Blintzes 149

Cherries

Bing Cherry Shortcakes 22

Brandied Cherries 21

Cherries 20

Cherry-Pineapple Freeze 55

Old-Fashion Cherry Pie 96

Red, White and Gooey Banana Splits
34

Strawberry Cobbler 116

Cherries 20

Cherries Jubilee 156

Cherries Jubilee In A Flash 157

Cherry Delight 31

Cherry Trifle 260

Cherry-Cream Tortes 263

Cherry-Nut Cake 247

Cherry-Pineapple Freeze 55

Chess Cake 242

Chilled Chocolate Mocha Pie 102

Chilled Pumpkin Souffle 83

Chocolate

Almond Custard with Chocolate Sauce
62

Amaretto Pot de Creme au Chocolate 70

Banana-Cream Cheese Pie 100

Chilled Chocolate Mocha Pie 102

Chocolate Cheesecake on Brownie Crust 111

Chocolate Cream 69

Chocolate Creme Brulee 71

Chocolate Marshmallow Ice Cream Pie 41

Chocolate Shells 141

Chocolate Souffles 81

Chocolate Tartlet Shells 142

Chocolate-Chocolate Gelato 53

Chocolate-Coconut Pie 100

Chocolate-Filled Cream Puffs 130

Creamy Chocolate Mousse 74

Creme de Menthe Pie 103

Crispy-Topped Pudding 58

Dark, Rich Chocolate Ice Cream 39

Easy Chocolate Sauce 08

Frozen Mocha Ganache 45

Heavenly Mocha Ganache Bites 129

Hot Fudge Sauce 9

Irish Cream Delight 104

Mint Chocolate Creme Anglaise 68

Phyllo Chocolate Triangles 125

Raspberry Crowned Chocolate Mousse in Ladyfinger Ring 72

Red, White and Gooey Banana Splits 34

Solo Chocolate Pies 101

Strawberries in Chocolate Tuxedos 24

Strawberry-Cream Cheese Pie 90

Chocolate Cheesecake on Brownie Crust 111

Chocolate Cookie Sunday 176

Chocolate Cream 69

Chocolate Creme Brulee 71

Chocolate Crepes 151

Chocolate Marshmallow Ice Cream Pie 41

Chocolate Sauce 266

Chocolate Shells 141

Chocolate Souffles 81

Chocolate Tartlet Shells 142

Chocolate Truffles 217

Chocolate-Apricot Torte 265

Chocolate-Cherry Cake 238

Chocolate-Cherry Cookies 175

Chocolate-Chocolate Gelato 53

Chocolate-Coconut Pie 100

Chocolate-Covered Strawberries 210

Chocolate-Dipped Stuffed Dates 219

Chocolate-Filled Cream Puffs 130

Chocolate-Peanut Clusters 216

Chocolate-Raspberry Pavlova 148

Cinnamon-Orange Custard 59

Cinnamon-Sugar Palmiers 188

Cobblers

Apple Crisp 118

Apricot Cobbler 113

Berry Blue Cobbler 115

Blueberry Hill Crunch 113

Express Fruit Cobbler 114

Lickity-Split Apple Crisp 119

Lightning Fast Peach Cobbler 115

Peach Crumb 118

Peachy-Amaretto Crunch 117

Special Peach Crisp 116

Strawberry Cobbler 116

Coconut

Butter Pecan-Pumpkin Parfait 43

Chocolate-Coconut Pie 100

Crispy-Topped Pudding 58

Peanut Butter Sauce 16

Pina Colada Sorbet 50

Coconut Bites 177
Coconut Crunch 16
Coconut Rounds 191
Coconut Sweets 227
Coconut-Chocolate Drops 178
Cookies
Almond-Meringue Cookie 183
Amaretti 187
Bourbon Balls 192
Brown Sugar Cookies 167
Butter Pecan Cookies 169
Butter Pecan Dreams 168
Butterscotch Haystacks 162
Butterscotch Sweets 163
Charlie McRoons 180
Chocolate Cookie Sunday 176
Chocolate-Cherry Cookies 175
Cinnamon-Sugar Palmiers 188
Coconut Bites 177
Coconut Rounds 191
Coconut-Chocolate Drops 178
Disappearing Cookies 164
Easy Sand Tarts 160
Easy Sugar Cookies 165
Fast Chocolate Macroons 181
Kiss Me Chocolate 177
Ladyfingers 182
Meringues 184
Mexican Wedding Cookies 161
Mocha-Chocolate Chip Meringues 185
Oatmeal-Chocolate Chip Cookies 179
Old-Fashion Peach Cookies 171
Orange-Pecan Cookies 170
Palmiers 190
Peanut Butter Chip Cookies 174
Peanut Butter Cookies 173
Peanut Butter Surprise Cookies 174
Peanutty Chocolate Tortillas 186

Pecan Balls 193
Potato Chip Crunchies 160
Snappy Almond -Sugar Cookies 166
Snowballs 191
Super-Fast Peanut Butter Drops 172
Cool Strawberry Pie 92
Cranberry
Cranberry-Chardonnay Sorbet 49
Cranberry-Chardonnay Sorbet 49
Cranberry-Coffee Cake 259
Cream Cheese-Strawberry Bars 205
Creamy Chocolate Mousse 74
Creamy Fruit Topping 13
Creamy Lemon Pie 99
Creamy Orange Chiffon 250
Creamy Peach Parfait Topped With
Almonds 84
Creamy Pecan Pie 107
Creamy Pecan Squares 197
Creamy Sunshine Cake 235
Creamy Surprise Cake 244
Cremes
Creme de Menthe Pie 103
Maple Creme Brulee 65
Creme de Menthe Pie 103
Creole Pralines 224
Crepes
Black Forest Crepes 153
Chocolate Crepes 151
Dessert Crepes 150
Fresh Strawberry Crepes 152
Crepes Suzette 154
Crispy Chocolate Bars 203
Crispy Peanut Butter Bars 198
Crispy-Topped Pudding 58
Crunchy Caramel-Topped Cheesecake 112
Crunchy Pecan Bites 211
Currants 123

Custard Filling 131

D

Dark, Rich Chocolate Ice Cream 39
Dates 219
Deluxe Coconut Cake 251
Dessert Crepes 150
Disappearing Cookies 164

E

Easy Apricot Trifle Express 261
Easy Blonde Brownies 199
Easy Cheesecake 112
Easy Chocolate Dessert Fondue 228
Easy Chocolate Sauce 08
Easy Creamy Chocolate Torte 266
Easy Fast Fudge 214
Easy Gooey Turtle Bars 202
Easy Graham Cracker Crust 109
Easy Nutty Bars 196
Easy Sand Tarts 160
Easy Sugar Cookies 165
Easy, Breezy Lemonade Pie 108
Everyday Special Brownies 200
Express Fruit Cobbler 114

F

Famous Flaming Desserts 155
Fancy Pound Cake 232
Fast Chocolate Macaroons 181
Flaming Desserts
    Bananas Foster 155
    Cherries Jubilee 156
    Cherries Jubilee In A Flash 157
    Crepes Suzette 154
    Island-Volcano Flambo 158
Floating Islands 61
Flourless Chocolate Cake 240

Fondue, Easy Chocolate Dessert 228
Fresh Berry Cake 246
Fresh Fruit With Hawaiian Glaze 33
Fresh Lemon Tarts 137
Fresh Lime Sherbet 47
Fresh Peach Tarts 136
Fresh Strawberry Crepes 152
Fresh Strawberry Mousse 78
Frosting, Chocolate-Cherry Cake 238
Frozen Desserts
    Butter Pecan-Pumpkin Parfait 43
    Cantaloupe Sherbet 48
    Cherry-Pineapple Freeze 55
    Chocolate Marshmallow Ice Cream Pie 41
    Chocolate-Chocolate Gelato 53
    Cranberry-Chardonnay Sorbet 49
    Dark, Rich Chocolate Ice Cream 39
    Fresh Lime Sherbet 47
    Frozen Mocha Ganache 45
    Granita 36
    Grape Granita 52
    Ice Cream 36
    Icy Pineapple Freeze 54
    Layered Ice Cream Treat 42
    Old-Fashion Ice Cream 38
    Orange Sorbet 51
    Peach Sherbet 47
    Pina Colada Sorbet 50
    Raspberry Sherbet 46
    Sherbet 36
    Sorbet 36
    Sweet Apricot Alaska 44
    Toffee Ice Cream Delight 40
Frozen Mocha Ganache 45
Fruit
    Apple-Spiced Pears 28
    Bing Cherry Shortcakes 22

Brandied Cherries 21
Cherry Delight 31
Cherry Cream Torts 263
Chocolate-Apricot Torte 265
Fresh Fruit With Hawaiian Glaze 33
Honeyed Pears 29
Not-So-Sweet Dessert Salad 32
Pears Poached in Wine 30
Red, White and Gooey Banana Splits
    34
Stained Glass Salad 31
Strawberries in Chocolate Tuxedos 24
Strawberries Topped with Sweetened
    Mascarpone 23
Sugared Peaches with Sweet Marsala
    Wine Sauce 27
Wine-Soaked Nectarines 26

Fudge
Layered Ice Cream Treat 42
Toffee Ice Cream Delight 40

G
German Chocolate Brownie Bars 201
Glaze, Chocolate-Cherry Cookies 175
Golden Butter Cake 237
Golden Rum Cake 242
Grandma's Strawberry Cake 253
Granita 36
Granite 36
Grape Granita 52

H
Hawaiian Glaze 33
Hawaiian Pineapple Cake 247
Heavenly Mocha Ganache Bites 129
Hello Dollies 194
Honeyed Pears 29
Honey-Glazed Apple Turnovers 120

Hot Fudge Sauce 9
Hot Spiced Apples Topping 14

I
Ice Cream
Butter Pecan-Pumpkin Parfait 43
Chilled Chocolate Mocha Pie 102
Chocolate Marshmallow Ice Cream Pie
    41
Frozen Mocha Ganache 45
Granita 36
Granite 36
Ice Cream 36
Layered Ice Cream Treat 42
Old-Fashion Ice Cream 38
Red, White and Gooey Banana Splits
    34
Sorbet 36
Sweet Apricot Alaska 44
Toffee Ice Cream Delight 40
Ice Cream 36
Icy Pineapple Freeze 54
Irish Cream Delight 104
Island-Pineapple Sauce 15
Island-Volcano Flambe 158

K
Kiss Me Chocolate 177

L
Ladyfingers
Layered Ice Cream Treat 42
Raspberry Crowned Chocolate
    Mousse in Ladyfinger Ring 72
Ladyfingers 182
Layered Ice Cream Treat 42
Layered Strawberry-Lemon Cake 236

Lemons

Creamy Lemon Pie 99
Easy, Breezy Lemonade Pie 108
Fresh Fruit With Hawaiian Glaze 33
Lemon Curd 77
Lemon Curd Mousse with Blackberry
    Sauce 76
Sunny Lemon Sauce 15

Lemon Cloud Bars 196
Lemon Curd 77
**Lemon Curd Mousse with Blackberry Sauce
    76**
Lemon Pound Cake 233
Lemon-Raspberry Parfaits 87
Lemony Cheese Tarts 138
Lemony Sponge Cake 234
Lickity-Split Apple Crisp 119
Lightning Fast Peach Cobbler 115
Limes

Fresh Lime Sherbet 47
Lime-Cheesecake Tarts 139

Lime-Cheesecake Tarts 139

M

Macaroons

Honeyed Pears 29

Maple Creme Brulee 65
Melon

Cantaloupe Sherbet 48

Meringues 184
Mexican Wedding Cookies 161
Microwave Pecan Brittle 226
Mini-Pumpkin Cakes 257
Mint Chocolate Creme Anglaise 68
Mint Special 56
Mocha-Chocolate Chip Meringues 185
Mom's Pound 230

Mousse

Cappuccino Mousse 79
Creamy Chocolate Mousse 74
Fresh Strawberry Mousse 78
Lemon Curd Mousse with Blackberry
    Sauce 76
Mousse 70
Raspberry Crowned Chocolate
    Mousse in Ladyfinger Ring 72
Sunny Citrus Mango Mousse 75

Mousse 70

N

Nectarines

Raspberry-Nectarine Tart 134
Wine-Soaked Nectarines 26

Not-So-Sweet Dessert Salad 32
Nuts

Almond Custard with Chocolate Sauce
    62
Apple Dumplings 122
Apricot Cobbler 113
Butter Pecan-Pumpkin Parfait 43
Candied Almond Topping 17
Cherry Delight 31
Chocolate-Coconut Pie 100
Creamy Peach Parfait Topped With
    Almonds 84
Creamy Pecan Pie 107
Honey-Glazed Apple Turnovers 120
Hot Spiced Apples Topping 14
Not-So-Sweet Dessert Salad 32
Old-Fashion Pecan Pie 107
Peachy-Amaretto Crunch 117
Peanut Butter Sauce 16
Phyllo Chocolate Triangles 125
Red, White and Gooey Banana Splits
    34

Strawberry Cobbler 116
Warm Walnut Sauce 18
Nut Truffles 218
Nutty Orange Logs 207

O

Oatmeal-Chocolate Chip Cookies 179
Old Southern Praline Sauce 230
Old-Fashion Applesauce Cake 245
Old-Fashion Blueberry Pie 98
Old-Fashion Cherry Pie 96
Old-Fashion Ice Cream 38
Old-Fashion Peach Cookies 171
Old-Fashion Peach Pie 97
Old-Fashion Pecan Pie 107
Oranges
    Cenci 128
    Cherry Delight 31
    Island-Pineapple Sauce 15
    Not-So-Sweet Dessert Salad 32
    Orange Sorbet 51
    Orange Souffles 82
    Stained Glass Salad 31
    Sunny Citrus Mango Mousse 75
Orange Glaze 256
Orange Sorbet 51
Orange Souffles 82
Orange-Pecan Cookies 170

P

Palmiers 190
Parfaits
    Almond Custard with Chocolate Sauce 62
    Amaretto Pot de Creme au Chocolate 70
    Blueberry and Pudding Parfaits 88
    Chilled Chocolate Mocha Pie 102

Chocolate Cheesecake on Brownie Crust 111
Chocolate Creme Brulee 71
Chocolate-Chocolate Gelato 53
Chocolate-Coconut Pie 100
Creamy Chocolate Mousse 74
Creme de Menthe Pie 103
Crispy-Topped Pudding 58
Hot Fudge Sauce 9
Irish Cream Delight 104
Lemon-Raspberry Parfaits 87
Phyllo Chocolate Triangles 125
Strawberries in Chocolate Tuxedos 24
Pastries
    Honey-Glazed Apple Turnovers 120
    Apple Dumplings 122
    Cenci 128
    Chocolate-Filled Cream Puffs 130
    Custard Filling 131
    Heavenly Mocha Ganache Bites 129
    Peach Phyllo Rolls with Caramel Sauce 126
    Phyllo Chocolate Triangles 125
    Phyllo Dough 124
    Quick and Easy Apple Pastries 123
    Tarte Tatin 133
Pavlovas 146
Peaches
    Berry Blue Cobbler 115
    Creamy Peach Parfait Topped With Almonds 84
    Lightning Fast Peach Cobbler 115
    Old-Fashion Peach Pie 97
    Peach Creme Brulee 66
    Peach Crumb 118
    Peach Phyllo Rolls with Caramel Sauce 126
    Peach Sherbet 47

Peachy-Amaretto Crunch 117
Special Peach Crisp 116
Stained Glass Salad 31
Sugared Peaches with Sweet Marsala
    Wine Sauce 27
Peach Creme Brulee 66
Peach Crumb 118
Peach Phyllo Rolls with Caramel Sauce 126
Peach Sherbet 47
Peaches n Cream 249
Peachy-Amaretto Crunch 117
Peanuts
Peanut Butter Sauce 16
Peanutty Ice Cream Crunch 16
Peanut Butter Chip Cookies 174
Peanut Butter Cookies 173
Peanut Butter Sauce 16
Peanut Butter Surprise Cookies 174
Peanutty Chocolate Tortillas 186
Peanutty Ice Cream Crunch 16
Pears
Honey Pears 29
Stained Glass Salad 31
Pears Poached in Wine 30
Pecan Balls 193
Pecan Bites, Crunchy 211
Pecan Toffee 220
Phyllo Chocolate Triangles 125
Phyllo Dough 124
Pies
Banana-Cream Cheese Pie 100
Chilled Chocolate Mocha Pie 102
Cool Strawberry Pie 92
Creamy Lemon Pie 99
Creamy Pecan Pie 107
Creme de Menthe Pie 103
Easy Graham Cracker Crust 109
Easy, Breezy Lemonade Pie 108

Irish Cream Delight 104
Old-Fashion Cherry Pie 96
Old-Fashion Peach Pie 97
Old-Fashion Pecan Pie 107
Old-Fashion Blueberry Pie 98
Snappy Strawberry Pie 93
Solo Chocolate Pies 101
Strawberry Fluff Pie 91
Strawberry-Cream Cheese Pie 90
Strawberry-Fruit Pizza 109
Strawberry-Strawberry Pie 94
Strawberry-Yogurt Pie 95
Sweet Potato Pie 105
Toffee-Caramel Pie 106
Pina Colada Sorbet 50
Pineapple
Apricot Cobbler 113
Blueberry Hill Crunch 113
Cherry-Pineapple Freeze 55
Easy, Breezy Lemonade Pie 108
Fresh Fruit With Hawaiian Glaze 33
Icy Pineapple Freeze 54
Island-Pineapple Sauce 15
Not-So-Sweet Dessert Salad 32
Pina Colada Sorbet 50
Stained Glass Salad 31
Sunny Lemon Sauce 15
Pineapple Upside-Down Cake 258
Poppy Seed Cake 255
Potato Chip Crunchies 160
Pound Cake A La Blueberries 231
Puddings
Almond Custard with Chocolate Sauce
    62
Blancmange 64
Cinnamon-Orange Custard 59
Crispy-Topped Pudding 58
Floating Islands 61

Rice Pudding with Boysenberry Sauce 60

Pumpkin
Butter Pecan-Pumpkin Parfait 43
Chilled Pumpkin Souffle 83
Pumpkin-Rum Cake 256

Q

Quick and Easy Apple Pastries 123
Quick and Easy Fruitcake 253
Quick Chocolate Bites 213
Quick Sticky Buns 209

R

Rainbow Cookie Ribbons 195
Raspberry Crowned Chocolate Mousse in Ladyfinger Ring 72
Raspberry
Lemon-Raspberry Parfaits 87
Raspberry Crowned Chocolate Mousse in Ladyfinger Ring 72
Raspberry Sauce 11
Raspberry Sherbet 46
Raspberry-Nectarine Tart 134
Wine-Soaked Nectarines 26
Raspberry Sauce 11
Raspberry Sherbet 46
Raspberry-Nectarine Tart 134
Red, White and Gooey Banana Splits 34
Rice Pudding with Boysenberry Sauce 60
Rocky Road Bars 204
Rum Sauce 12

S

Sauces
Blackberry Sauce 76
Boysenberry Sauce 10
Caramel Sauce 127
Caramel Sauce 9
Creamy Fruit Topping 13
Easy Chocolate Sauce 08
Hawaiian Glaze 33
Hot Fudge Sauce 9
Hot Spiced Apples Topping 14
Island-Pineapple Sauce 15
Peach Phyllo Rolls with Caramel Sauce 126
Raspberry Sauce 11
Rum Sauce 12
Sunny Lemon Sauce 15
Whipped Cream 13
Whiskey Cream 14
Sherbert
Cantaloupe Sherbet 48
Fresh Lime Sherbet 47
Peach Sherbet 47
Sherbet 36
Snappy Almond-Sugar Cookies 166
Snappy Strawberry Pie 93
Snowballs 191
Snowy Almond Fudge 215
Solo Chocolate Pies 101
Sorbet
Chocolate-Chocolate Gelato 53
Cranberry-Chardonnay Sorbet 49
Grape Granita 52
Orange Sorbet 51
Pina Colada Sorbet 50
Sorbet 36
Souffles
Chilled Pumpkin Souffle 83
Chocolate Souffles 81
Orange Souffles 82
Souffle 80
Souffle 80
Special Peach Crisp 116

Stained Glass Fudge 212
Stained Glass Salad 31
Sticky Cinnamon Rolls 208
Strawberries
  Cool Strawberry Pie 92
  Fresh Strawberry Mousse 78
  Red, White and Gooey Banana Splits
    34
  Snappy Strawberry Pie 93
  Stained Glass Salad 31
  Strawberries in Chocolate Tuxedos 24
  Strawberries Topped with Sweetened
    Mascarpone 23
  Strawberry Cobbler 116
  Strawberry Fluff Pie 91
  Strawberry-Cream Cheese Pie 90
  Strawberry-Fruit Pizza 109
  Strawberry-Strawberry Pie 94
  Strawberry-Topped Cheesecake 110
  Strawberry-Yogurt Pie 95
Strawberries in Chocolate Tuxedos 24
Strawberries Topped with Sweetened
    Mascarpone 23
Strawberries, Chocolate-Covered 210
Strawberry Cobbler 116
Strawberry Fluff Pie 91
Strawberry Pavlova 146
Strawberry-Cream Cheese Pie 90
Strawberry-Fruit Pizza 109
Strawberry-Lemon Curd Tartlets 145
Strawberry-Strawberry Pie 94
Strawberry-Topped Cheesecake 110
Strawberry-Upside Downs 254
Strawberry-Yogurt Pie 95
Strawberry-Zabaglione Tarts 143
Sugared Peaches with Sweet Marsala Wine
    Sauce 27
Sunny Citrus Mango Mousse 75

Sunny Lemon Sauce 15
Super Oreo Cake 239
Super-Fast Peanut Butter Drops 172
Sweet Apricot Alaska 44
Sweet Potato Pie 105

T
Tarts
  Black Walnut-Maple Tartlets 144
  Caramel-Pecan Tarts in Chocolate Shells
    140
  Chocolate Shells 141
  Chocolate Tartlet Shells 142
  Chocolate-Raspberry Pavlova 148
  Fresh Lemon Tarts 137
  Fresh Peach Tarts 136
  Lemony Cheese Tarts 138
  Lime-Cheesecake Tarts 139
  Raspberry-Nectarine Tart 134
  Strawberry Pavlova 146
  Strawberry-Lemon Curd Tartlets 145
  Strawberry-Zabaglione Tarts 143
Tarte Tatin 133
Tarts 135
Toffee
  Banana Crunch Parfaits 85
  Toffee Ice Cream Delight 40
  Toffee-Caramel Pie 106
Toffee Crunch 18
Toffee Ice Cream Delight 40
Toffee-Caramel Pie 106
Toffee-Meringue Torte 264
Topping
  Crunchy Caramel-Topped Cheesecake
    112
  Hawaiian Glaze 33
  Red, White and Gooey Banana Splits
    34

Toffee Crunch 18
Topping, Buttery Walnut Squares 206
Tortes 262
Cherry-Cream Tortes 263
Chocolate-Apricot Torte 265
Easy Creamy Chocolate Torte 266
Toffee-Meringue Torte 264
Turbinado Sugar 189

V

Very Merry Berry Pie 95

W

Walnut Maples 223
Warm Walnut Sauce 18
Whipped Cream 13
Whipping Cream
Almond Custard with Chocolate Sauce 62
Banana Crunch Parfaits 85
Bing Cherry Shortcakes 22
Caramel Sauce 9
Chilled Pumpkin Souffle 83
Chocolate Cheesecake on Brownie Crust 111
Chocolate Cream 69
Cool Strawberry Pie 92
Creamy Chocolate Mousse 74
Creamy Fruit Topping 13
Creme de Menthe Pie 103
Dark, Rich Chocolate Ice Cream 39
Easy, Breezy Lemonade Pie 108
Easy Creamy Chocolate Torte 266
Easy Chocolate Sauce 08
Fresh Strawberry Mousse 78
Frozen Mocha Ganache 45
Heavenly Mocha Ganache Bites 129

Irish Cream Delight 104
Lemon Curd Mousse with Blackberry Sauce 76
Lemon-Raspberry Parfaits 87
Mint Chocolate Creme Anglaise 68
Mint Special 56
Not-So-Sweet Dessert Salad 32
Old-Fashion Ice Cream 38
Peanutty Ice Cream Crunch 16
Raspberry Crowned Chocolate Mousse in Ladyfinger Ring 72
Rum Sauce 12
Snappy Strawberry Pie 93
Strawberries Topped with Sweetened Mascarpone 23
Strawberry Fluff Pie 91
Strawberry-Strawberry Pie 94
Strawberry-Yogurt Pie 95
Sunny Citrus Mango Mousse 75
Toffee-Caramel Pie 106
Very Merry Berry Pie 95
Whipped Cream 13
Whiskey Cream 14
White Chocolate-Mocha Mousse Parfaits 86
Whiskey Cream 14
White Chocolate-Mocha Mousse Parfaits 86
Wine-Soaked Nectarines 26

Grocery List

FRUIT

___ Apples
___ Apricots
___ Bananas
___ Bing Cherries
___ Blackberries
___ Blueberries
___ Boysenberries
___ Cherries
___ Cranberries
___ Currants
___ Fruit
___ Grapes
___ Kiwi
___ Lemons
___ Lime
___ Mango
___ Melons
___ Nectarines
___ Oranges
___ Peaches
___ Pears
___ Pineapple
___ Raspberries
___ Strawberries

LIQUOR

___ Amaretto
___ Apricot Brandy
___ Bourbon
___ Brandy
___ Chardonnay
___ Cherry liqueur
___ Creme de cacao liqueur
___ Creme de menthe
___ Curacao
___ Irish Cream Liqueur
___ Marsala wine
___ Orange Liqueur
___ Raspberry Liqueur
___ Riesling Wine
___ Rum
___ Whiskey
___ Zinfandel Wine

FRESH BAKERY

___ Bread
___ Cake
___ Cookies
___ Croissants
___ Muffins
___ Pastries
___ Pies
___ Rolls

DAIRY

___ Biscuits
___ Butter
___ Cheese
___ Cottage Cheese
___ Cream Cheese
___ Eggs
___ Half-and-Half
___ Juice
___ Lemon Curd
___ Margarine
___ Milk
___ Orange Juice
___ Sour Cream
___ Whipping Cream
___ Yogurt

FROZEN FOODS

___ Pound Cake
___ Bread Dough
___ Cheesecake
___ Brownies, Ready-to-use
___ Pastry Sheets
___ Puff Pastry
___ Sugar cookie dough
___ Phyllo dough
___ Tart shells
___ Chocolate shells
___ Whipped topping

GROCERY

___ Almond extract
___ Almonds, slivered
___ Aluminum foil
___ Angel food cake
___ Apple pie spice
___ Applesauce
___ Apricot jam
___ Apricot pie filling
___ Baking powder
___ Baking soda
___ Biscuit mix
___ Blueberry pie filling
___ Blueberry quick-bread
    mix
___ Boysenberry sauce
___ Butter
___ Butter cookies
___ Butterscotch chips
___ Cake mix
___ Candy bars
___ Caramel sauce
___ Caramels
___ Cereal
___ Cherry pie filling
___ Chocolate chips
___ Chocolate Milk
___ Chocolate, bittersweet
___ Chocolate, milk toffee
    bits
___ Chocolate, semi-sweet
    baking squares
___ Chocolate, white
    baking
___ Chow mein noodles
___ Cinnamon
___ Cinnamon-spice oatmeal
___ Cloves
___ Cocoa
___ Coconut, flaked
___ Corn starch
___ Corn syrup
___ Cranberry sauce
___ Cream of coconut

GROCERY

- ___ Crescent dinner rolls
- ___ Dates
- ___ Evaporated milk
- ___ Flour
- ___ Frosting
- ___ Fudge topping
- ___ Gelatin, unflavored
- ___ Ginger ale
- ___ Graham crackers
- ___ Honey
- ___ Instant coffee
- ___ Instant pudding mix
- ___ Jelly
- ___ Ladyfingers
- ___ Lemon extract
- ___ Lemon pie filling
- ___ Macaroons
- ___ Mandarin oranges
- ___ Maple syrup
- ___ Maraschino cherries
- ___ Marshmallow creme
- ___ Marshmallows
- ___ Mayonnaise
- ___ Nutmeg
- ___ Orange chiffon cake
- ___ Oil
- ___ Parchment paper
- ___ Peach pie filling
- ___ Peaches, canned
- ___ Peanut butter
- ___ Peanut butter chips
- ___ Peanuts
- ___ Pears, canned
- ___ Pecans
- ___ Pie crust
  - ___ Chocolate
  - ___ Graham crackers
  - ___ Shortbread
  - ___ Chocolate cookie
  - ___ Mini-graham cracker
- ___ Pineapple, chunks
- ___ Pineapple, crushed
- ___ Pineapple, tidbits

GROCERY

- ___ Pineapple pie filling
- ___ Popcorn
- ___ Poppy seeds
- ___ Potato chips
- ___ Powdered sugar
- ___ Pudding
- ___ Pudding and pie filling
    mix
- ___ Pumpkin pie filling
- ___ Pumpkin pie spice
- ___ Quick-cooking oats

GROCERY

- ___ Nuts/Seeds
- ___ Popcorn
- ___ Raisins
- ___ Rice
- ___ Salt
- ___ Seasonings
- ___ Shortening
- ___ Sodas
- ___ Spices
- ___ Sponge cakes
- ___ Strawberry pie filling
- ___ Strawberry preserves
- ___ Sugar, brown
- ___ Sugar, light brown
- ___ Sugar, white
- ___ Sweet potatoes
- ___ Sweetened condensed
    milk
- ___ Tea
- ___ Tortillas
- ___ Vanilla extract
- ___ Vanilla wafer
- ___ Vinegar
- ___ Walnuts
- ___ Water
- ___ Wax paper

OTHER

- _____
- _____
- _____
- _____
- _____
- _____
- _____
- _____
- _____
- _____
- _____
- _____
- _____
- _____
- _____
- _____
- _____
- _____
- _____
- _____
- _____
- _____
- _____
- _____
- _____
- _____
- _____
- _____

Pie Pans

Pan Sizes	Approximate Volume
7 x 1½	2 cups
8 x 1¼	3 cups
8 x 1½	4 cups
9 x 1¼	4 cups
9 x 1½	5 cups
10 x 2	6 cups

Cake Pans

Pan Sizes	Approximate Volume
5 x 2 round	2⅔ cups
6 x 2 round	3¾ cups
8 x 1½ round	4 cups
7 x 2 round	5¼ cups
8 x 2 round	6 cups
9 x 1½ round	6 cups
9 x 2 round	8 cups
9 x 3 bundt	9 cups
10 x 3½ bundt	12 cups
9½ x 2½ springform	10 cups
10 x 2½ springform	12 cups
8 x 3 tube	9 cups
9 x 4 tube	11 cups
10 x 4 tube	16 cups

Here is a simple chart that makes conversion from U.S. measurements to metric as easy as pie.

1 teaspoon	5 ml
2 teaspoons	10 ml
1 tablespoon	15 ml
2 tablespoons	30 ml
1 cup	237 ml
2 cups = 1 pint	473 ml
3 cups	710 ml
4 cups = 1 quart	.95 liter
4 quarts = 1 gallon	3.8 liters
1 ounce	28 grams
2 ounces	57 grams
3 ounces	85 grams
4 ounces	113 grams
6 ounces	170 grams
8 ounces	227 grams
16 ounces = 1 pound	454 grams
2.2 pounds	1 kilogram

FORMULAS

To Convert, Multiply What You Know By:

Cups to liters	x .236
Cups to milliliters	x 236.6
Gallons to liters	x 3.8
Ounces (fluid) to milliliters	x 29.6
Ounces (weight) to grams	x 28.4
Pints to liters	x .47
Pounds to kilograms	x .45
Quarts to liters	x .95
Tablespoons to milliliters	x 14.8
Teaspoons to milliliter	x 4.9

COOKBOOKS PUBLISHED BY COOKBOOK RESOURCES

Easy Cooking With 5 Ingredients

The Ultimate Cooking With 4 Ingredients

The Best of Cooking With 3 Ingredients

Easy Gourmet Cooking With 5 Ingredients

Healthy Cooking With 4 Ingredients

Easy Slow-Cooker Cooking With 4 Ingredients

Easy Dessert Cooking With 5 Ingredients

Quick Fixes With Mixes

Casseroles To The Rescue

Kitchen Keepsakes/More Kitchen Keepsakes

Mother's Recipes

Recipe Keepsakes

Cookie Dough Secrets

Gifts For The Cookie Jar

Cookbook 25 Years

Pass The Plate

Texas Longhorn Cookbook

Mealtimes and Memories

Holiday Treats

Homecoming

Cookin' With Will Rogers

Best of Lone Star Legacy Cookbook

Little Taste of Texas

Little Taste of Texas II

Southwest Sizzler

Southwest Ole

Classroom Treats

Leaving Home

To Order **Easy Desserts Cooking With 5 Ingredients**:

Please send_____ copies @ $19.95 (U.S.) each $_____

Plus postage/handling @ $6.00 each $_____

Texas residents add sales tax @ $1.45 each $_____

Check or Credit Card (Canada-credit card only) **Total** $_____

Charge to my ☐ *VISA*   or   ☐ MasterCard.

Account #_____

Expiration Date_____

Signature_____

Mail or Call:
Cookbook Resources
541 Doubletree Drive
Highland Village, TX 75077
Toll-free: 866/229-2665
972/317-0245
www.cookbookresources.com

Name_____

Address_____

City_____State_____Zip_____

Phone (day)_____ (night)_____

— —

To Order **Easy Desserts Cooking With 5 Ingredients**:

Please send_____ copies @ $19.95 (U.S.) each $_____

Plus postage/handling @ $6.00 each $_____

Texas residents add sales tax @ $1.45 each $_____

Check or Credit Card (Canada-credit card only) **Total** $_____

Charge to my ☐ *VISA*   or   ☐ MasterCard.

Account #_____

Expiration Date_____

Signature_____

Mail or Call:
Cookbook Resources
541 Doubletree Drive
Highland Village, TX 75077
Toll-free: 866/229-2665
972/317-0245
www.cookbookresources.com

Name_____

Address_____

City_____State_____Zip_____

Phone (day)_____ (night)_____

To Order **Easy Desserts Cooking With 5 Ingredients**:

Please send_____ copies @ $19.95 (U.S.) each $_____

Plus postage/handling @ $6.00 each $_____

Texas residents add sales tax @ $1.45 each $_____

Check or Credit Card (Canada-credit card only) **Total** $_____

Charge to my ☐ **VISA** or ☐ **MasterCard**

Account #_____

Expiration Date_____

Signature_____

Mail or Call:
Cookbook Resources
541 Doubletree Drive
Highland Village, TX 75077
Toll-free: 866/229-2665
972/317-0245
www.cookbookresources.com

Name_____

Address_____

City_____State_____Zip_____

Phone (day)_____ (night)_____

- -

To Order **Easy Desserts Cooking With 5 Ingredients**:

Please send_____ copies @ $19.95 (U.S.) each $_____

Plus postage/handling @ $6.00 each $_____

Texas residents add sales tax @ $1.45 each $_____

Check or Credit Card (Canada-credit card only) **Total** $_____

Charge to my ☐ **VISA** or ☐ **MasterCard**

Account #_____

Expiration Date_____

Signature_____

Mail or Call:
Cookbook Resources
541 Doubletree Drive
Highland Village, TX 75077
Toll-free: 866/229-2665
972/317-0245
www.cookbookresources.com

Name_____

Address_____

City_____State_____Zip_____

Phone (day)_____ (night)_____